To Anne:

Good Luck with the New Studio!

Love
Kathleen
& Evan ☺

Irreplaceable Artifacts

Irreplaceable Artifacts

DECORATING THE HOME WITH ARCHITECTURAL ORNAMENT

Evan Blum and Leslie Blum

Photographs by DAVID FRAZIER

CLARKSON POTTER/PUBLISHERS

NEW YORK

Published by Clarkson N. Potter, Inc./Publishers,
201 East 50th Street, New York, New York 10022.
Member of the Crown Publishing Group.

www.randomhouse.com

CLARKSON N. POTTER, POTTER, and colophon
are trademarks of Clarkson N. Potter, Inc.

Printed in Hong Kong

Design by Constance Old

Illustrations by Lydia Romero

Library of Congress Cataloging-in-Publication
Data is available upon request.

ISBN 0-517-70486-2

10 9 8 7 6 5 4 3

TO OUR PARENTS, who supported us in everything that we have attempted to do, and who stored the marquee for the Loew's Delancey Theater in their yard for two years.

CONTENTS

ORNAMENT, *when it is really creative, organic ornament, is the very perfume of the architectural flower. It is the smile of a sentiment, the last line in the sonnet.*

LOUIS H. SULLIVAN, <u>KINDERGARTEN CHATS</u>. SCARAB FRATERNITY PRESS, 1934

FOREWORD

Celebrated in the photographs of this book are the homes of creative individuals who, either by themselves or in conjunction with an architect or a designer, have found wonderful ways to incorporate pieces of salvaged architectural ornament—"irreplaceable artifacts"—into their lives. Very often they fell in love with a particular object while looking for something else. Sometimes they didn't know how they would use the artifact, but they rescued it or bought it anyway. Only later did they find the perfect spot in which to hang it or figure out how to make it into a table or a door or a headboard. In some cases, entire rooms were created around an architectural element or an ornament set the tone for other furnishings. In other instances, people looked long and hard before finding an object that perfectly expressed a vision or a feeling about their home.

Some ornamental details can be displayed on their own, as artwork, and a number of examples of this are presented here. These ornaments have great integrity in and of themselves. Hanging alone on a wall, they don't look out of place, like a stuffed lion's head from a safari, but rather more like a sculpture or a painting. A different approach is to incorporate an ornament or fragment into a larger piece, breathing new life into the artifact by finding a new use for it. Keystones or column capitals made into table bases, grilles made into headboards, window surrounds made into fireplace mantels: pieces that might look lost and out of context on their own may fit right in when given a new role. However they are reused, these ornaments have intrinsic value; they can give us pleasure and visually enrich our lives just as do paintings and sculptures. Some pieces shown in these pages were, in fact, crafted by classically trained sculptors or by workers who went on to become famous as artists. But most architectural ornaments were made by anonymous artisans who created folk art comparable to the weather vanes or quilts or furniture produced by other craftspeople. And like any folk art, we use these ornamental details because we wish our homes to be more expressive, more distinctive. Such irreplaceable artifacts allow us to create a unique environment.

Not so long ago architectural ornament from demolished buildings was considered trash. Among the best-known victims of this appalling disregard were the magnificent sculptures from New York's Pennsylvania Station, which ended up in a landfill in the New Jersey Meadowlands. Several tons of ornament from the Cable and Republic Building in Chicago were dumped into Lake Michigan. Masses of detail from lesser buildings were disposed of without a second thought. It is unthinkable that any other art form would have been so callously thrown away, but the reality is that we have lost an enormous part of our architectural heritage and with it, the magnificent ornament, often including one-of-a-kind objects that will never be replicated.

Fortunately the growing interest in recycling has added to the appeal of salvaging architectural detail. Finding new uses for rescued artifacts now makes enormous sense economically as well as aesthetically. Creatively integrating salvaged building material—which includes not only ornament but also doors, windows, lighting fixtures, and flooring—into new construction has become an important tenet of the "green" design movement. Reuse of these items keeps them out of the landfills that are already strained by our disposable society.

In addition, salvaging and reutilizing these elements reduces our need to use new resources and additional energy. Using old wood doors, for example, saves trees, the gasoline used by trucks that transport the wood, and the energy needed to craft new doors. The production of metal ornament is particularly energy-intensive, from the mining of the raw materials to the forging of the finished product. Further, the quality of the workmanship and the material used in rescued ornament is generally of a very high quality that would be difficult, and would certainly be very expensive, to replicate today. Quite frequently a rescued detail or element is much less expensive and far more appealing than a comparable one that is new, even factoring in the cost of restoring the old piece.

Most architectural details look good and work well indoors or out. The advantage of using an element that was originally part of a building's facade in a garden is that the piece can, with only minimal care, last for years. While some pieces will require restoration or repair, many can be used in the condition in which they were found. Rust, weathering stains, minor cracks or crazing, and even peeling paint can add to the charm of an architectural element, depending on the material, the owner's taste, and the final use. Because of the tremendous increase in the preservation of historic buildings, there are now many qualified craftspeople who are knowledgeable about historic ornament and can assist in cleaning and repairing artifacts. In addition, there is a proliferation of books and periodicals that offer useful information about caring for materials in place on an old building that can apply equally well to rescued elements.

Building ornament offers a tangible link to the past, a reminder of an era in architecture that contrasts sharply with our own. The twentieth century witnessed a dramatic change in architectural style from buildings that were richly ornamented to structures with little or no decoration. Many of us yearn for the detail and scale that these embellishments provided, and we find their reuse in the home enormously satisfying. Artifacts can also evoke memories that link us to personal experiences: a pedestal sink may remind us of the one in our grandparents' bathroom, a keystone may look like one that hung over the doorway of our first school, or a fireplace might resemble the one in the lodge where we spent our family vacations. We cannot own all these buildings from our past, nor do we necessarily have the power to preserve them. But we *can* own an object that connects us to our individual and collective history, that attaches us to a cherished memory. And by finding new uses for these architectural details, we can create new art forms, acknowledging their historical value but imparting to them an immediacy that takes them beyond nostalgia to enrich our lives, today and tomorrow.

HISTORY

THE DESIRE TO REUSE ARCHITECTURAL ORNAMENT HAS AT ITS ROOTS THE

same urge that motivates the historic preservation movement—to save our architectural heritage for future generations. If an entire building cannot be preserved intact, then we should at least make our best effort to save the ornament that represents the workmanship of talented artisans and embodies the visual aesthetics of a particular era. There is no doubt that ornament looks best on the building for which it was intended, where its material, color, shape, and scale work with all of the other building elements as a whole. If, as the architect Mies van der Rohe said, the whole, in architecture, is greater than the sum of its parts, what then is the value of an individual part separate from the whole? Taken out of context, an individual piece of

Previous page: The 1961 demolition of the proscenium and stage of the Garrick Theater in Chicago, built by Adler and Sullivan.

Like many of the buildings designed by the architectural firm of McKim, Mead and White, Penn Station, above, was built to last a thousand years, but did not make it to the end of this century. Its demolition in 1963–65 prompted the New York Times *to write, "We want and deserve tin-can architecture in a tin-horn culture. And we will probably be judged not by the monuments we build but by those we have destroyed."*

ornament is always diminished. If a sculpture by Rodin were to be divided into its parts—an arm here, a leg there—the parts would be interesting but would not have the impact of the complete sculpture. But if only a few parts of a Rodin could be rescued, saving them would be preferable to losing the entire sculpture. Similarly, if a structure must be demolished or altered—and despite our best efforts to preserve as much of value as possible, there will always be buildings that cannot be saved intact—then every effort should be made to salvage those elements that are significant. Luckily, some details can stand on their own, especially when applied to a new use that takes advantage of their special qualities. And many artifacts are so beautiful, crafted with such care and with such design integrity, that even independent of their original structure they are stunning.

While we have lost some important and beautiful buildings to fire and to natural disasters, the vast majority of the buildings that are no longer standing today were demolished by owners who saw no more use for them. As Richard Nickel, the architectural photographer who helped lead the efforts in Chicago during the 1960s and early 1970s to save the city's significant buildings, said, "Great architecture has only two natural enemies: water and stupid men."

No building type has been spared; government buildings, housing, commercial structures, and houses of worship alike have fallen victim to the wrecker's ball. In every part of the country and in every city at one time or another, important buildings and neighborhoods have been leveled in the name of progress. All of America's greatest early architects and engineers have had at least one of their works demolished; in the case of some, numerous buildings have been lost. Richard Morris Hunt, George B. Post, Henry Hobson Richardson, Frank

The Second City Comedy Club in Chicago incorporates the second floor loggia from the demolished Garrick Theater by Adler and Sullivan into its facade. While not a substitute for preserving the original building, this at least allows an important piece of the city's architectural history to remain and be enjoyed by its citizens.

Furness, William Le Baron Jenney, James Bogardus, Burnham & Root, McKim, Mead and White, Louis Sullivan, and Frank Lloyd Wright all designed wonderful buildings that were important pieces in the history and development of American architecture and that are now gone. Countless other buildings, designed by lesser architects, or without architects but containing nonetheless wonderful examples of the style and craft of a particular era, and forming the fabric of older neighborhoods, have also been demolished.

European countries have been much more advanced than the United States in preserving their important architecture. In the 1830s the French architect Viollet-le-Duc was commissioned to restore many of France's most important and beautiful buildings. In England, William Morris's Society for the Protection of Ancient Buildings was created well before the end of the nineteenth century. Yet no federal laws concerning building preservation existed in the United States until 1906, when Congress passed the Antiquarian Act. This marked the first phase of preservation in this country: saving buildings because of their historic value. The homes of famous people and buildings where important events had occurred began to be saved from ruin or destruction, especially if the person or event had taken place long enough ago to have acquired the sheen of history. There was no consideration, however, for the aesthetic, architectural, or urban planning role that a building played. As Thomas Stauffer, one of the leaders of the losing battle to save Adler and Sullivan's Garrick Theater in Chicago in 1960, rather forcefully complained after the building was demolished, "If Lincoln [had] taken a piss in the Garrick, we would have had no problem saving the building."

The second phase of preservation in the United States took place in the 1920s and 1930s with the establishment of self-contained museum villages that re-created an era. Of these, Williamsburg, Virginia, developed by John D. Rockefeller, and Greenfield Village in Michigan, built by Henry Ford, were the earliest and remain the best known. People don't actually live in these towns; they are, instead, attempts to recapture the sense of bygone days. Although they may contain some original buildings, many of the structures are contemporary reconstructions. Museum villages fulfill an educational need to understand how people lived in earlier times, and allow us to satisfy a nostalgic hunger for images of a quaint and simpler life. But they present a selective history that is closer to Disneyland than to a real and vibrant city.

In the United States, where "newness" has always been synonymous with "progress," buildings of a previous era have time and again been torn down to make room for new buildings. But the scale of destruction reached a peak during the 1950s and 1960s, when our older urban areas fell into disfavor and entire downtown neighborhoods were leveled in the name of urban renewal. During these years public policy encouraged the new and abandoned the old; it spurred development in the suburbs at the expense of traditional downtowns.

What is appalling now in retrospect is the number of truly historic and magnificent buildings that were torn down to make way for parking lots and highways: Frank Lloyd Wright's Larkin Building in Buffalo, the Provident Life and Trust Company in Philadelphia by Frank Furness, Adler and Sullivan's Garrick Theater Building in Chicago, and the Chicago and Northwest Railway Passenger Depot by Charles Sumner Frost in Milwaukee, to name a few of the most famous. In the 1930s the Historic American Buildings Survey was undertaken to document the nation's architecture, primarily those structures built prior to 1830. By the early 1960s almost 25 percent of the listed buildings had been demolished, a level of destruction that does not take into account the even greater losses of buildings dating from the late 1800s and early 1900s.

In May of 1965 a White House Conference on Natural Beauty laid the groundwork for the most important piece of preservation legislation ever to be passed by the United States Congress: the National Historic Preservation Act of 1966. This act expanded the definition of what was considered worthy of preservation to include sites with aesthetic value or with historic or cultural value on a state or local level, as well as those with purely historic national importance. In addition, it provided tools and techniques—among them, matching funds—to actively encourage preservation activities, including the acquisition and restoration of properties. That same year Congress also passed the Department of Transportation Act, which required federal transportation planning to take into consideration the potential impact of projects on natural areas and historic sites, and the Model Cities Act, which provided funding for the identification, acquisition, and restoration of historic properties.

This legislation, combined with local ordinances in cities that had lost one too many special buildings—buildings that were landmarks in that they marked the city, a location, an era, or a feeling about that city for its citizens—represented a turning point in historic preservation. Although a number of important buildings have been demolished since that time, the destruction has slowed considerably, especially since 1978, when the U.S. Supreme Court upheld the

This is one of a set of carved limestone caryatids that Irreplaceable Artifacts removed from a building at Madison Avenue and Sixty-first Street in Manhattan for the owner of the building just prior to its demolition. The two-and-one-half-ton figures now sit in the building owner's garden.

right of a municipality to designate and preserve important structures in its landmark ruling in *Penn Central Transportation Co. vs. City of New York.*

An inadvertent blow was delivered to preservation, and to building ornament in particular, by the passage of laws in many municipalities aimed at ensuring the structural integrity of all of the elements of a building's facade. Following a pedestrian's death after a piece of a building fell off, Chicago revised its building code in 1978 to include the critical examination of building facades and enclosures. New York enacted its own legislation in 1980 with Local Law 10 after a woman was killed by a piece of a building that came loose and fell on her. Many other cities followed suit. While the inten-

tion of these laws—to protect passersby from being struck by pieces falling from buildings—was certainly commendable, the impact on ornament was devastating. Rather than spend the money for a comprehensive analysis of the facade and then take the necessary precautions to ensure structural integrity, many building owners simply removed any portion of the building that projected from the facade. Cornices, balconies, gargoyles, and other ornamental elements were removed wholesale. Owners sometimes allowed the pieces to be carefully removed and salvaged, but often they were simply destroyed.

The use of architectural salvage is, of course, not new. All civilizations have reused materials from demolished buildings. In this country, numerous mansions and town houses built at the end of the nineteenth and the beginning of the twentieth centuries integrated elements from buildings in Europe. Rich patrons actually sent scouts to scour Europe for architectural elements such as doors, mantels, stained-glass windows, and even entire rooms that could be utilized in their homes. The fact that an item came from a château in France or a church in Germany conferred upon it a certain luster, reflecting a general feeling among the elite in the United States that European art and architecture were superior to what was available at home. The most flamboyant and well publicized of these treasure hunters was William Randolph Hearst, who used myriad pieces that had been removed from buildings abroad to beautify San Simeon, his estate in California. Unlike the examples shown in this book, however, Hearst's salvaged elements were reused in

This classic Atlantic City hotel, the Blenheim, one of the great ladies of a past era, was demolished by a technique called implosion, which speeds up the process but that makes ornamental salvage all but impossible.

the way in which they were originally intended; they were not converted into a new and different use.

One exception to the general disregard for local ornament was Abram S. Hewitt, the mayor of New York City from 1887 to 1888. He was the son-in-law of Peter Cooper, the tycoon who founded the Cooper Union for the Advancement of Science and Art in Manhattan. Hewitt, who was also an ironmaster, inherited from Cooper a magnificent estate in Ringwood, New Jersey. It was there that he installed pieces of ornament from New York buildings, including twelve Ionic columns from the old New York Life Insurance Building, gates and light fixtures from the English governor general's home, twelve iron tochères on stone pedestals from Colonnade Row on Lafayette Street, iron gates from the old Columbia College at Madison Avenue and Forty-ninth Street, a set of gates from the Charles William Cooper house on Twenty-first Street and another pair of gates from the William Waldorf Astor mansion that had sat on the site of the Empire State Building.

No one today knows how exactly he acquired these items, although most experts believe that he just fancied them and decided to take them. Now on display at the old New Jersey estate, which is part of Ringwood State Park, these items were joined more recently by two statues from Penn Station in New York City, demolished in 1965. The statues—two of eight female figures representing Day and Night carved by Adolph Weinman—had been buried in a dump in the Jersey Meadowlands, where they were found by a young boy who was sure he had discovered the lost continent of Atlantis. The two statues were moved to Ringwood State Park; a third statue of Night, the only other one recovered from the landfill, is displayed at the Brooklyn Museum.

What is unique about the era after World War II in this country is that we have torn down build-ings with magnificent ornament and replaced them with buildings that have little or no ornament. In 1966, Ada Louise Huxtable, the architecture critic for the *New York Times,* lamented, "The landmark invites the wrecker and its replacement reduces the public image to the lowest possible common denominator. Architecture has ceased to be a noble art. But it only serves man's needs and aspirations, and men and cities get what they deserve."

Although many outstanding modern buildings have been constructed since the end of World War II and talented architects are working today, our environment is becoming ever more bland and mediocre, devoid of the grace notes supplied by ornament. A former director of the Brooklyn Museum, Thomas Buechner, has said that "our city is being extruded, rolled out and poured into blank-faced forms … in spite of having more hands and more time and more knowledge than ever before in the history of the world, we live in a time of the clean line, the metaphysical proportion, the very, very empty space." The consequence of this architectural denuding is that many of us feel an almost desperate need to rescue as much ornament as possible, both because of its inherent beauty and because we need to fill the void created by much of our recently built environment.

Surely there are individuals in every city who have rescued one or many pieces of ornament. Perhaps they passed a demolition site and saw a carved keystone in a pile of rubble ready to be thrown away. Somehow they figured out a way to rescue that keystone and get it home. Or maybe they were walking past a Dumpster and peered in only to find a segment of a cast-iron stair railing that tickled their fancy. They hauled it out of the Dumpster and found a place to use it in their home. For some individuals, salvaging became a passion, perhaps an obsession.

In New York City, Ivan Karp began saving ornament in the 1950s when, during his strolls around the city, he realized how many buildings with lovely ornament were being demolished. Working with his wife, Marilynn, and a dedicated group of like-minded citizens known as the Anonymous Arts Recovery Society, he rescued close to four thousand pieces of ornament over the course of forty years. On behalf of the society, he donated many of these pieces to museums around the country and eventually founded the only museum in the United States dedicated to architectural ornament.

In Chicago, architectural photographer Richard Nickel fell in love with the work of Louis Sullivan, considered the father of modern architecture in America. During the 1950s and 1960s, when Sullivan's work was being routinely abandoned or demolished, Nickel got caught up in the efforts to document the buildings while they still stood, to try to save them from destruction, and then to salvage the ornament from the ones that couldn't be saved. He rescued many pieces just before the arrival of vandals or wreckers. Eventually acknowledged for this work, he was hired by the city of Chicago in 1960 to photograph several important buildings prior to their demolition and then to salvage the significant ornament. Elements that he rescued are in museums across the nation. Southern Illinois University at Edwardsville has several hundred such pieces on display and hundreds more in storage. Nickel's final salvage effort, that of the Chicago Stock Exchange in 1972, led to his death when a portion of the building collapsed on him after he had returned one night to retrieve several last items that he coveted. His story, and that of architectural loss in Chicago, is wonderfully told in the book *They All Fall Down* by Richard Cahan.

Over the years a number of enlightened demolition contractors recognized the value of the structures they were tearing down and saved interesting pieces for their own enjoyment and for possible resale. But in the fifties and sixties there was little demand for these pieces, and so the quantity of ornament that could be saved often depended on the size of a contractor's yard; most of it was carted off to the dump. By the early 1970s, however, a market had begun to appear for salvaged ornament, especially pieces that had been retrieved from important buildings by well-known architects. Many museums started to realize the importance of the ornament, and their interest helped to fuel the market. As the seventies progressed, the value of ornament increased to the point where fine pieces were being stolen from vacant, and in some cases even from occupied, buildings in poorer urban areas. In addition to the actual thievery involved, these were acts of terrible vandalism, since many ornamental pieces have structural as well as aesthetic value. When keystones and window surrounds are removed from a building, for instance, the loss seriously compromises the building's structural integrity, almost dooming it to destruction rather than rehabilitation. By the early 1980s all major cities had at least one dealer in architectural salvage, and the media had begun to pick up on the trend, with articles on the subject appearing in magazines and newspapers.

The reuse of architectural ornament in new ways found special favor with restaurants, nightclubs, and hotels. These gathering places are always looking for a theme that will distinguish one from the next. The presence of elements from, say, an old train station, a post office, or a movie theater provides instant ambience and noteworthiness. A single demolished building might yield twenty keystones, fifty doors, and two hundred feet of cornice. Few homes can accommodate decorative elements in this quantity, but restaurants and hotels often can, and in doing so they get a unified visual motif. In addition, the scale of some architectural pieces is better suited to spaces larger than those that exist in most homes, and these oversize pieces deliver an enormous visual impact.

It was against this background that Irreplaceable Artifacts, one of the nation's largest dealers in rescued architectural ornament, was founded in New York City in 1977. While our business officially is salvaging and dealing in architectural ornament, we believe that we are recycling culture—the culture of the people who came to America and built its cities. In the beginning, our operation rather resembled an adoption agency for homeless artifacts, as we struggled to find families for these pieces. We sought out potential users, and we helped owners, architects, and interior designers discover new ways to incorporate them into their projects. But besides selling ornament, we have become expert at salvaging it. Our projects include the Commodore, Biltmore, and Vanderbilt hotels; the Loew's Delancey, Loew's Paradise, and New Yorker movie theaters; the Helen Hayes Theater; a Horn and Hardart Automat; the Audubon Ballroom; the Candler Building; and the New York Life Insurance Building—all in New York City. In Chicago we removed ornament from 900 North Michigan Avenue, from 10 and 134 South LaSalle Street, and from the Armory Building. We have dismantled numerous town houses and mansions, including the Wrightsman Estate in Palm Beach and the Biddle mansion in Blue Bell, Pennsylvania, and the material we have rescued has been used in restaurants and hotels around the world, even in such far-flung spots as the Peak Café in Hong Kong.

The Century Cafe in New York's Theater District uses the marquee from the Loew's Delancey movie theater to form an impressive backdrop for its bar, which gives the restaurant a strong visual identity.

The skills necessary for salvaging ornament are not necessarily those needed for demolishing a building. To do a good job one must have a thorough understanding of building construction and materials, a knowledge of heavy rigging, and a love of the ornament. Sometimes the job also requires strong back and legs, as when workers for Irreplaceable Artifacts had to remove forty sea monsters from the rooftop terraces of New York's Candler Building on West 42nd Street and carry these three-hundred-pound terra-cotta sculptures down twenty-three flights of stairs in order to rescue them.

While demolition contractors often receive money for the items that get salvaged or for the building's salvage rights, the payment is usually minuscule compared to the cost of the actual demolition and carting away of the remains. Salvage work is also almost always done under pressure, literally one step ahead of the wrecker's ball. Despite a flourishing market for salvage, many items are still lost today because of the time it takes to remove certain pieces, and demolition contracts usually have heavy penalty clauses to ensure speedy performance.

Brooklyn Museum's Frieda Schiff Warburg Memorial Sculpture Garden gives visitors the opportunity to enjoy the anonymous art of architectural details and to reflect on the immensity of what our neighborhoods have lost.

When the Diplomat Hotel (formerly the Elks Club) on West Forty-third Street in New York City was demolished, Irreplaceable Artifacts was able to salvage fourteen of its copper-plated cast-iron balconies (see photograph page 56), but there was not enough time to rescue over 10,000 square feet of magnificent ornamental plaster.

An exception to the thoughtless urgency so often demonstrated in tearing down buildings was found with the Helen Hayes Theater in New York, where one of the conditions established by the New York City Landmarks Preservation Commission allowing the demolition of this glorious theater was the careful removal of the ornament. Irreplaceable Artifacts sadly agreed to do the work (we had been actively involved in efforts to preserve the building), removing chandeliers, seats, murals, and some of the city's most beautiful plaster ornament.

While most museums around the country have period rooms and perhaps a few pieces of ornament, only a handful of museums have extensive collections. Foremost among these is the Brooklyn Museum, which has the largest collection of rescued exterior architectural ornament in the world. Inaugurated in April 1966, the Frieda Schiff Warburg Memorial Sculpture Garden displays over three hundred pieces of rescued stone carvings, terra-cotta castings, and exterior metalwork from buildings that were demolished or renovated; the museum has several thousand additional pieces in storage. Roughly 75 percent of the collection was donated by the Anonymous Arts Recovery Society (see page 30). The rest was donated by demolition contractors, developers, and just ordinary folk who had found and saved pieces of ornament. Donations from other parts of the country include a pair of cast stone corbels from San Francisco and a keystone from the Four Deuces Club in Chicago; the New York City treasures include six column capitals from Louis Sullivan's Bayard Building, zinc lions from the old Steeplechase Park in Coney Island, and the figure of Night, a ten-foot-high sculpture in pink granite that originally sat atop New York's Penn Station.

When it became apparent that the Chicago Stock Exchange by Adler and Sullivan could not be preserved, the Chicago Art Institute arranged to salvage the heart of the building, its magnificent Trading Room, and to reconstruct it as part of the museum's new East Wing. A very faithful restoration was done, largely based on photographs taken by Richard Nickel. Dismantling the room took approximately eleven weeks. During the process, the salvagers were thrilled to discover that about 75 percent of the stained-glass skylights were intact and that the supporting cast-iron mullions could be demounted. During reconstruction, which began in March of 1976, workers reused as many elements as possible and painstakingly re-created what was missing. The institute also rebuilt the terra-cotta archway from the Stock Exchange's main entrance to mark its entrance from Columbus Drive. In addition, a collection of ornamental fragments from other buildings, called "Fragments of Chicago's Past," is on permanent exhibition in the institute's Henry Crown Gallery.

The Wolfsonian Foundation, which houses the Mitchell Wolfson Jr. collection of nineteenth-and twentieth-century art and design, went one step further in its headquarters in Miami Beach. When a 1927 landmark warehouse was recently converted to house the organization, elements from the collection acquired over the years were integrated into the new building. In the main entrance hall, behind a newly constructed reflecting pool and fountain, the foundation installed a portion of the green-and-gold terra-cotta facade of a 1929 movie theater from Norristown, Pennsylvania, composed of over two hundred stylized glazed terra-cotta tiles that were saved prior to demolition. Windows, panels, and frames from the same theater have been reused in the second-floor conference room. The unqiue polychrome wooden ceiling and brass chandeliers from a Miami automobile showroom were installed in the seventh-floor gallery space, and thirteen bronze column circlets from the same showroom were used to make table bases in the curatorial offices. The flagpoles and mounts from the Biltmore Hotel in New York City, which were rescued by Irreplaceable Artifacts, were incorporated into the front of the building. In all, close to twenty different kinds of architectural items were used in new ways in the museum, and the Wolfsonian's creative design marks a significant advance in the display of rescued ornament: not as an object from a forgotten past but as a useful component of the present.

While the destruction of our architectural heritage has certainly slowed in recent years, buildings will continue to be demolished or renovated, and rescued ornament will need to find new homes. There is certainly no reason to relegate these details to the trash heap of our collective history.

And so this book is a celebration of the inventive ways in which architectural artifacts can be reused. There are no rules here—you are free to mix materials, periods, and styles. Each time you reuse an architectural detail, you are breaking new ground. The challenge is to use these elements in ways different from those for which they were originally intended, to create a new art form out of an old one. From the smallest fragment to the largest frieze, you can take a piece of history and make it a part of your life. And as you look through these pages, remember also to look up and around at your own town and to appreciate the irreplaceable decorative details of the architecture that still remains.

THE ANONYMOUS ARTS MUSEUM

Nestled among the rolling hills of Schoharie County in Upstate New York sits the only museum in the world devoted entirely to the display of architectural ornament rescued from demolished buildings. The Anonymous Arts Museum opened in 1985, but its origins go back to 1950, when Ivan Karp, the museum's founder, discovered his first architectural carving, a cherub's face in terra cotta, resting in a pile of rubble on a demolition site in lower Manhattan. "Glancing up," he

View of the interior of the Anonymous Arts Museum. The terra-cotta horse's head in the lower right is a recent acquisition of the museum. The piece was removed from one of the last remaining riding stables in Brooklyn in 1995.

recalls, "I could see with what abandon and disdain the demolition people were proceeding to take down the building with its ornament. And knowing that they didn't care one way or another whether I picked up this cherub, I took it home." This was to be the first of over four thousand

The basement of the Anonymous Arts Museum, left, holds a cache of several hundred pieces awaiting display.

These number plaques, right, identified the different stands at the Washington Market in lower Manhattan. At the bottom of the display is a "spite cat." When the building that this came from was first constructed, the neighbors were vehement in their dislike of it. The owner placed a series of these cats on the building to spite the neighbors.

decorative elements that he would eventually rescue. He realized that if he continued to walk through neighborhoods where demolition crews were active, mostly on the Lower East Side of Manhattan, he might find other carvings. "These fabulous carvings were coming down all around us, and nobody cared," moans Karp, obviously experiencing once again the dismay he'd felt at the time.

The smaller terra-cotta items he could carry off by hand, but larger stone carvings were beyond him. He tried shopping carts, he borrowed a car, he even tried rolling heavy objects on pipes as had the ancient Egyptians. Fortunately he was able to recruit two like-minded friends with time on their hands, and they "would go around picking up stones."

In most instances when a stone ornament falls from a building, especially a piece of terra cotta, it gets chipped or bruised or loses a critical feature like a nose. So the three friends started asking crew members to lower the ornament down instead of just throwing it to the ground. In certain cases a polite request would work; they would negotiate with the foreman and usually give him a little money. But since Karp and his friends were out of work at the moment—that was why they had the time to do this work—it wasn't easy to come up with the money. This led them to decide that they could salvage the material just as well themselves, as long as the scaffolding around the building was up. So, working at twilight or dawn or on Sundays, the trio

became expert at salvaging stone carvings. They would carry the pieces (occasionally, Karp was able to persuade his father to lend him his car) to the Brooklyn backyard of one of the cohorts; the yard quickly filled up with stone satyrs and gremlins, lions and maidens.

They also enlisted the help of their wives and girlfriends, whom they dubbed "rubble molls," to distract night watchmen and police officers. Sometimes the ploy didn't work. "One chilly night a watchman caught us and threatened to call the police," Karp recollects. "I handed him ten dollars and said in my most menacing voice 'Here, go out and get drunk or we'll tie you up.' Needless to say, he took the money." They were even arrested once, charged not with trespassing or larceny but with "laboring on a Sunday," this being the era when the blue laws were still in effect in New York. Karp says, "After I explained our purpose to the desk sergeant, he scolded the policeman for his lack of culture and told us to pursue our noble labors. We would have anyway."

They started to call themselves the Sculpture Rescue League, which was not an official name, but proved to be helpful. As Karp recounts, "We would be up in a building removing the ornament and someone would yell up to us, 'Hey, you there! What are you doing?' And we would yell back, 'We're the Sculpture Rescue League.' The passerby would nod and say, 'Oh, okay,' and continue on his way." It was decided, however, that the name sounded too political, even a bit conspiratorial. The next name they came up with was Rubble Without Applause, which had great conversational value and a certain charm yet did not convey the seriousness with which they viewed their mission. They finally settled on

the Anonymous Arts Recovery Society, which became incorporated as a not-for-profit organization in 1958.

Around that time, and after they had collected close to five hundred pieces, the wife of the associate with the backyard finally insisted that she wanted her yard back. As they began the search for a place to store their cache of ornament, they heard that the Brooklyn Museum had some space where they stored building equipment.

Karp approached the museum's director, Thomas Buechner, about accepting this collection of anonymous art. "At first, Buechner didn't understand exactly what we were offering him," recalls Karp. "What do you mean, rubble?" asked Buechner. "Not rubble, but anonymous art—fine carvings, uncelebrated carvings, that we are losing forever," responded Karp. Beuchner looked at a few examples and agreed that "it was good stuff and a shame to throw away."

Over the next five or six years the AARS brought close to fifteen hundred pieces to a grassy area behind the Brooklyn Museum. There was, unfortunately, no maintenance money during the early years, and Karp estimates that about 25 percent of the pieces were lost to the destructive forces of nature. In 1966, however, the museum inaugurated the Frieda Schiff Warburg Memorial Sculpture Garden to display a portion of the donated ornament. The most fragile pieces are in a small building that protects them from the elements, and the bulk of the collection is in storage.

When, in 1969, he opened the O. K. Harris Gallery in Manhattan, Karp took advantage of space in the gallery's basement to store close to a thousand pieces. The gallery also held a num-

These magnificent carvings display an extraordinary level of craftsmanship, which truly qualifies them as anonymous art.

ber of exhibits of architectural ornament, and the AARS sold duplicates to help support the organization. Over the years the AARS also donated salvaged ornament to the Cooper-Hewitt National Design Museum, the Museum of the City of New York, and the Museum of the State of New York.

In 1984, Karp and his wife, Marilynn, a professor of art history at New York University, acquired an 1860s former general store on Main Street in Charlotteville, New York, a small town west of Albany. They renovated the wood-frame building and created two museums, which opened to the public in 1985. On the ground floor is the Anonymous Arts Museum, displaying the most beautiful, interesting, and rare pieces that the AARS has rescued over the years. On the second floor is the Charlotteville Museum, where the history of the town is preserved in photographs, artifacts, and oral histories; both are open to visitors only during summer weekends.

Although he is no longer actively scouting for and salvaging artifacts, Ivan Karp still gets interesting pieces of architectural ornament from people who are familiar with his reputation. His most recent acquisition, a terra-cotta horse's head in three-quarters profile, was salvaged in 1994 from one of last remaining riding stables in Brooklyn; it is now on display at the museum. Karp truly believes, and has spent over forty years acting on the belief that saving architectural ornament is, in his own words, "a major poetic act."

METAL

FROM THE RED-GOLD LUSTER OF POLISHED BRASS TO THE CRUSTY BLACK OF

old cast iron, metal has a sensuality that makes it endlessly appealing. Hammered,

wrought, cast, extruded, or stamped, it forms voluptuous curves, crisp lines, or

playfully naive motifs. The ease with which metal can be worked into useful and

decorative elements has given it throughout history a premier place among the

materials used for architectural ornament.

The earliest extant architectural use of metal is found in cast-bronze casings

for wooden doors in the Pantheon in Rome, dating from approximately A.D.124.

Since that time, each of the metals has had its vogue over the years, depending on

the fashion and the availability of raw materials. Starting in the second half of the nineteenth and continuing into the beginning of the twentieth century, technological improvements spurred the development of new alloys and improved production methods, thereby reducing manufacturing costs and allowing an ever widening range of applications.

Until the appearance of cast-iron buildings in the late 1800s, metal ornament generally had no structural use; it served merely to decorate or protect. Well suited to a defensive or protective use, it could be fabricated either to allow access to light, air, and views or to keep out the elements. Fences, railings, grilles, gates, posts, and roofs as well as cornices and crestings, doors, and hardware were the dominant decorative uses of metal. With the rise of the use of cast iron, however, entire buildings began to be constructed from metal and then shipped to a building location and assembled on site.

Today many neighborhoods gain their character from their distinctive metal ornament, from the once gritty industrial districts with cast-iron facades to graceful row house communities with cast-iron and wrought-iron window grilles, stair railings, and fencing. Indeed, some of our greatest architectural treasures are distinguished by their ingenious display of the metalworker's art.

BRASS AND BRONZE

Bronze and brass have traditionally been considered the noblest of the architectural metals. This status is due in large part to the high level of detail that can be captured in the two metals. Bronze, the alloy that has been longest known and used, is a compound of copper, zinc, and tin, whereas brass is an alloy of just copper and zinc. Historically, the two are almost inseparable; many early pieces thought to be bronze, when analyzed with modern techniques, turned out to be brass, and vice versa.

The significant difference is that bronze, thanks

Previous page: Cast-iron stoop railings and fences in Gramercy Park, New York City.

When this apartment, opposite, was connected with an adjoining apartment, a new hallway was created to give access to the living room, and the doorway that once opened onto the living room was no longer necessary. But the owners wanted to retain a sense of openness and a visual connection to the room, and so they thought of installing a leaded-glass window. When they saw this grille, originally the central panel of the entrance doors from the Biba department store in London, they realized that it would allow air as well as light to pass. Since the grille was smaller than the original doorway, they built in a window seat below the opening and then constructed a support frame, aligning it with the pattern of the grille. The pattern is also echoed in the flooring and the ceiling molding.

to the addition of tin, is more resistant to corrosion and acquires a more uniform patina. Most architectural ornaments, especially those intended for exterior use, were therefore fabricated from bronze. Brass was more often chosen for its color and the high polish that could be achieved than for its corrosion resistance. Entrance doors, window grilles, elevator gates, teller wickets, ticket booths, stair railings, mailboxes, movie marquees, and decorative plaques and friezes are the most common bronze and brass items that can be found today. Lighting fixtures and hardware were as likely to be made from one alloy as from the other, and both metals were also used extensively to plate cast iron.

The most common method of making bronze and brass ornament was by casting, either in sand or using a technique known as *cire perdue* (lost wax). Both of these methods allow the metal to capture minute detail; sand casting was preferred for heavy relief, while *cire perdue* was more appropriate where a design had many undercuts. Brass and bronze ornament could also be wrought or hammered, but this was a more expensive process.

The natural color of polished bronze is a luminous warm gold. The rich nutty brown often associated with architectural bronze is acquired by atmospheric oxidation after long exposure, combined with proper cleaning procedures; a wide range of browns and greens can be more quickly achieved through the use of chemicals known as oxidizing agents. But regardless of method and color, the color change in bronze occurs only on the surface of the metal—unlike rust on iron, which eats away the material—since oxidation affects the first millimeter or so of the bronze and then stops, preventing any further corrosion.

Brass can vary in color depending upon the proportion of zinc or the addition of minute amounts of other metals. For example, a high proportion of zinc will give the brass a very yellow cast; a small amount of aluminum will produce a brass that is a light gold; a bit of manganese will cause a more bronzelike color; and the addition of nickel (to create nickel silver) will yield a silvery sheen.

IRON

Iron, either cast or wrought, is the most ubiquitous of the architectural metals. Never considered a noble material, it nonetheless has left its stamp on our architectural heritage. Iron fences, gates, balconies, doors, grilles, and railings adorn buildings and gardens across the country, and the visual identity of cities like New Orleans, Charleston, and Savannah is closely associated with the fanciful iron railings, balconies, and verandas that grace the facades of their nineteenth-century buildings.

The earliest ornamental ironwork was wrought—in other words, it was bent, hammered, twisted, flattened, or stretched, with or without heat. This was a handcrafted process, often resulting in visible hammer marks and irregularities that added to the artistic quality of a piece. And as it was

The conversion of this wrought-iron gatepost into a standing lighting fixture was relatively simple. An elongated 60-watt showcase bulb about 12 inches long was installed on a walnut base screwed into the four corners of the post. An opalescent glass cylinder was then placed over the bulb in the center of the post. A walnut cap was made to cover the light; it comes off to give access to the bulb.

worked and reworked to achieve the desired shape, the material actually became stronger.

By the nineteenth century wrought-iron products were widely available through catalogs, and some architectural historians believe that these catalogs were responsible for popularizing the decorative use of wrought iron, especially in the South. In the twentieth century wrought iron has occasionally been plated in nickel or copper, in whole or in part, and embellished with brass, copper, or enameled ornaments. The best craftsmen mixed wrought and cast iron, and they worked the iron in the repoussé method. Wrought-iron articles are often custom-made even today, and the finest examples by twentieth-century master blacksmiths such as Samuel Yellin rival bronze in their elegance and ornamentation.

The iron used for wrought work has less than one percent carbon content, making it more resilient and malleable than the iron used for casting. For this reason wrought iron was used first for structural bars, pins, and tie rods and later for I beams, where tensile strength is important. Its lower carbon content also makes wrought iron somewhat more resistant to rust, although the metal was often painted when used outdoors. The preferred finish, for both interior and exterior use, was created by baking the iron in a heavy coat of linseed oil. This resulted in a transparent finish that enhanced the variations in color and texture caused by working the metal.

Cast iron holds a unique position in the history of American architecture and urban development. The techniques for producing cast iron were refined, and the production costs were thereby reduced, at a time when American cities were booming in response to the industrial revolution. From the 1840s to the early 1900s, hundreds of iron-fronted commercial and retail buildings were constructed in cities

To create a see-through doorway between a kitchen and a dining room, the architect installed these wrought-iron elevator doors, which came from the Astor Apartments on New York City's Upper West Side, designed by Clinton and Russell in 1905. The openness of the design on the doors creates a sense of separation without closing off one space from the other. Stock double-acting door closers were attached to each door and to the floor and ceiling. These closers allow the doors to swing in either direction and to stay in the open or closed position on either side. The spring closure on the bottom was carefully fitted into the door and is completely independent of the frame. A redwood strip on the inside vertical edge of each door was added to make up the difference between the dimensions of the doors and the existing doorway opening.

Directly adjacent to New York's Grand Central Station, and designed by the same architectural firm, Warren and Wetmore, the Commodore was one of the city's premier hotels when it opened in 1920. Over the years, as the great age of rail travel gave way to the automobile, the hotel declined. In 1980 it became the Grand Hyatt, and in the course of refitting the hotel with a reflective glass facade, 150 of these copper masks were removed from the cornice. This mask now sits in an entry hall, complementing a Chinese chair and vase, and catching the sunlight as it once did atop the Commodore Hotel. Because the mask is made of repoussé sheet copper, it is relatively light, under 20 pounds. The horizontal cornice piece behind the mask is supported by a simple wooden frame made from 1-by-2-inch framing lumber, which is hung on picture hooks attached to the wall.

stairway from the Chicago Stock Exchange, designed by Adler and Sullivan in 1894. When the building was demolished, a section of the staircase was rescued and erected in the American Wing of the Metropolitan Museum of Art in New York City.

Residential buildings of the nineteenth century used cast iron extensively for decorative and security purposes. Intricate lintels could be cast in iron to adorn the windows on an otherwise simple masonry building, while cast-iron window grilles, fences, gates, and roof cresting on town houses offered almost lacelike details, often in contrast with the solidity of the background stone or brick. For the interior, hot-air registers and radiator covers were available from catalogs in a wide variety of shapes and sizes to match any style of decorating.

Since the carbon content of cast iron is higher than that of wrought iron, it is more brittle and more resistant to corrosion. It is also more fire-resistant and has a higher compressive strength, making it a suitable material for columns but not for beams. Cast iron for exterior use always has to be painted, although over the years the layers of paint can obliterate the detail. For interior use, cast iron was often heavily oiled, then baked at high temperature. When cool, it was greased, thus preserving the integrity of the details. Like wrought iron, it was occasionally plated in nickel, copper, bronze, or brass.

COPPER

Look up at the roofline of any city and you will see cooper in its ornamental roofs and in its cornices and gutters. When polished, copper has a warm red-gold glow; when allowed to weather, it quickly develops a distinctive green patina only a few millimeters deep. Over the centuries it has played a largely utilitarian role on buildings, mostly as a roofing material; a number of important American

buildings have copper roofs that have lasted for over two centuries. Occasional examples of more ornamental uses, such as copper-clad doors, knockers, or lighting fixtures, can also be found, and Victorian cast-iron hardware, stair railings, and newel posts were sometimes copper-plated.

The earliest ornamental use of copper in the United States was for weather vanes and statuary on the top of buildings and monuments. Its relative softness and malleability made it one of the least expensive building materials to work by hand. This, coupled with its ease of maintenance, made it the material of choice for cornices, cresting, spandrels, and other repetitive building components that were to be installed in relatively inaccessible places. A decorative design could be stamped at a reasonable cost, and lengths of stamped copper could then be welded or soldered together easily to provide a graceful finish to what might otherwise have been an unremarkable building. Once installed, copper oxidizes, creating the beautiful patina that protects the metal from further corrosion and renders seams virtually invisible.

Another less common and more artisanal method of working copper is called repoussé. This method has traditionally been used for custom-made ornaments and statuary, the most famous being the Statue of Liberty in New York Harbor.

The Otis Building on West Eighty-sixth Street was one of the first structures in New York City to be built as a cooperative residence. Constructed at the end of the 19th century, the building was renovated in the 1980s, and twenty-four cast-iron elevator doors were removed at that time. Two of the doors have been reused in this beautiful loft. The door on the left leads to the elevator, the one on the right to the fire stairs. Where the original doors had wire safety glass, these have been reglazed with frosted glass to allow the glow of the lights behind them to come through, while preserving privacy for the residents.

The Audubon Ballroom in New York's Harlem is probably best known today as the site where Malcolm X was assassinated. But it was originally part of one of New York's most beautiful movie palaces, the William Fox Audubon Theater. Designed in 1912 by the leading theater designer of the era, Thomas W. Lamb, it was covered with magnificent polychrome terra-cotta ornament and topped by an unusual zinc cornice. The building was demolished in 1994, but portions of the facade and the ballroom are being reincorporated into a new complex called the Audubon Research Park. A fragment of the salvaged zinc cornice is displayed as a piece of artwork in the hallway of this home. At the end of the panel, where a piece of the cornice is missing, a skillfully created trompe l'oeil version fills in.

In repoussé work, the craftsperson essentially models a sheet of copper with hammers and punches of various sizes, working and reworking it until the desired form is created. Because the French are the true masters of repoussé, when it came time to rebuild the Statue of Liberty in 1982, an entire crew of French metalworkers, Les Métalliers Champenois, was imported to replicate the most ornate and intricate portions of the job.

ZINC

The use of zinc for architectural purposes in this country is relatively recent. In France, Belgium, and Germany, it began to replace copper and lead in roofing in the early 1800s. In the United States, however, zinc in its pure form was never a common roofing material. Only with the invention of the galvanizing process in 1837, which allowed sheet iron to be coated with zinc to reduce corrosion, did its use became widespread. Galvanized sheet roofing was often stamped with designs, especially during the Victorian era, or formed to resemble a more expensive material like slate or terra cotta. Decorative roof crestings could also be formed

Two very distinct kinds of metal ornament have been used in this elegant dining room. An Art Deco cast-aluminum panel from a demolished commercial building in St. Louis has been integrated into the wooden wall paneling, displayed as if it were a painting. Adjacent to it is an Art Nouveau wrought-iron balcony from eastern France that has been made into a side table. Because the balcony railing weighs several hundred pounds, it has been secured to the wall and the floor to prevent it from falling over. The polished black granite tabletop sits on the railing and on a continuous piece of wood that matches the paneling.

in galvanized iron for considerably less than their cost in stone; these were generally purchased by the running foot from roofing-material catalogs.

Cast zinc, frequently sandblasted to imitate stone, was used extensively in the United States for cemetery monuments during the latter half of the nineteenth century. Many of these pieces can still be found remarkably well preserved, indeed often surviving better than actual stone monuments. Statues made of zinc were custom-cast to adorn important civic buildings and were also available through catalogs, which offered castings and formed pieces joined together. Architectural details such as brackets and scrolls to support cornices, column capitals, and medallions were often made of cast or stamped zinc, as were ornamental details that were added to embellish galvanized-iron cornices.

From the 1880s to about 1910, cornices, lintels, and other architectural elements as well as entire building facades were often made of pressed galvanized metal. Painted to imitate stone, wood, or cast iron, these pieces could be fabricated at a fraction of the cost and weight of the simulated materials. Designs ranged from the simplest to the most fanciful, with something available for every architectural style and taste.

TIN

Because tin is a very soft metal, it has played only a small role on its own in architectural ornament. Its most important use historically has been when alloyed with copper to form bronze; architectural bronze contains up to 10 percent tin, bell metal has around 25 percent tin, and "white bronze," which was once used for mirrors, could be up to one-third tin. More recently, tin has been used to plate iron and, later, steel sheets, mostly for roofing. Originally developed in Europe, tin roofs were noncombustible, relatively lightweight and quite durable, qualities

that so impressed Thomas Jefferson that he chose to install a tinplate roof at Monticello, his Virginia home. Although tinplate was first available in sheets for roofing, by the mid-1800s shingles pressed by machine were also being widely produced. These shingles could be made to replicate other, more costly materials; they might also incorporate designs that could be ingeniously formed to create the overlaps and interconnections necessary to make a roof watertight.

The decorative pressed ceilings commonly referred to as "tin ceilings" were, in fact, rarely made of tinplate; rather, they were usually painted sheet iron or steel. Tinplate was often put to ornamental use, however, in planters and urns, roof cresting and finials, stairway balusters, and lintels for doorways and windows.

LEAD

Lead, which is extremely soft and relatively easy to convert from an ore to a refined metal, was used by many early civilizations to make tools and ceremonial objects. Its first architectural uses were for roofing and related components such as downspouts, flashings, and gutters. These elements were sand-cast, sometimes with ornamental details such as crests or monograms. In the nineteenth century, sheet iron or steel was coated with a lead-tin alloy to produce a roofing material called terne, or terneplate, and this lead-tin alloy was also used occasionally to plate sheet copper for roofing. Purely decorative building elements made of lead, such as turrets, spires, finials, or crestings, became popular during the nineteenth century.

Because of its malleability, lead has played an important role in holding windowpanes in place ever since the twelfth century. The lead rods with H-shaped cross sections that serve to hold glass panes are known as cames. These lead rods can

During the height of the use of cast iron in architecture, a column capital like this one could be ordered from a catalog. It would be shipped in either two or four sections and then bolted together on-site. Shown here is a particularly decorative capital that has been cleaned and then lacquered to prevent rusting. The solidity of the iron contrasts beautifully with the airiness of the fern that it holds.

easily be worked around irregularly shaped pieces of glass and then soldered together at the point where two intersecting cames meet. Whether stained or clear, most ornamental glass in windows, doors, transoms, and skylights is surrounded by lead cames. Although zinc was often chosen for more geometric designs and, later in the twentieth century, copper and brass were also used, any window displaying very curvilinear designs most likely contains lead cames. Damage to stained- or leaded-glass panels can usually be traced to structural failure of the cames or of the solder holding them together.

Garden ornament and statuary were often made of lead, which does not rust or corrode when exposed to water. Nineteenth-century estates, for instance, frequently displayed lead fountains, urns, planters, flower boxes, and statuary in their gardens. Today many of these items have been salvaged and are available for use, but care must be taken not to place them where children or animals might come in contact with them or drink water from them because of the danger of lead poisoning.

STAINLESS STEEL

With a carbon content between wrought and cast iron, steel is stronger in both compression and tension than either form of iron, and so by the late 1800s it had come to replace iron, both cast and wrought, for structural purposes. Buildings were constructed with a steel framework that could support the entire weight of the building, thereby reducing the thickness of the exterior walls and increasing the usable, and rentable, floor area. This development ushered in the era of modern skyscrapers.

The use of steel for decorative purposes was never extensive, although it could occasionally be found in doors and window frames, stairways and banisters, balconies, elevator cages, and doors. Regardless of its use, the metal always had

Pinned to the wall to accentuate its delicacy and airiness, this polished cast-bronze demilune transom grille is truly a work of art. Its clean graphic lines and simple decoration work beautifully in this contemporary dining room. The grille was once over the entrance doors of the former Guggenheim Pavilion on East Seventy-second Street in New York City.

This ventilator grille graced the entrance lobby of 60 Wall Tower, built in 1932 by the architects Clinton and Russell, in lower Manhattan until it was removed during a renovation of the building. In 1978 the grille was featured in an exhibit at the Cooper-Hewitt Museum called "Ornament in the Twentieth Century." Its zigzag motif and the stylized flowers at its top and bottom are typical of the Art Deco style of the era. The dimensions of the grille perfectly matched those of a queen-size bed, so the owner adapted it to make a stunning headboard. The grille is relatively light because it is made of aluminum. Since it is attached to a sheetrock wall, however, its weight is supported by a half-inch strip of redwood that sits under it and is affixed to the studs behind the wall. A redwood frame that is rabbeted one-half inch on all four sides to overlap the edges of the grille was set around it and screwed into the wall behind the bed; the screw holes are covered with redwood plugs. The frame finishes the piece and at the same time holds it tight against the wall behind.

to be coated to inhibit rust. The earliest decorative pressed-metal ceilings known as tin ceilings were actually made of stamped sheet iron, but the later ceilings were fashioned from stamped sheet steel. In these uses, the steel was painted after being stamped, or it was galvanized with zinc for use outdoors or on porches.

In the beginning of the twentieth century, scientists developed a form of steel that would not corrode. They experimented with adding chromium or nickel, and then both metals, to steel, to produce the alloy now known as stainless steel. (Most stainless steels contain approximately 18 percent chromium and 8 to 12 percent nickel, depending upon the intended use.) Hard, ductile, with great tensile strength and resistance to corrosion, stainless steel is truly a versatile material: it can be worked

hot or cold, cast, forged, soldered, or welded. Its only drawback is its cost, which limits its use to those applications that require exceptional corrosion resistance.

As a decorative material, stainless steel can be polished to a high gloss and will retain that gloss indefinitely. This quality made stainless steel, in particular, along with other "white" metals such as aluminum and nickel, much in demand during the 1920s and 1930s, when a mirror polish reinforced the popular streamlined look. One of the greatest examples of Art Deco design is New York's Chrysler Building, where the entire upper third of the structure is clad in sheet stainless steel; the gargoyles that jut out from it are cast stainless steel, and the main entrance and storefronts are elegantly adorned with rolled sheets and extruded sections of stainless steel. The elevator doors, made of stainless steel inlaid with exotic wood to form stylized lotus blossoms, are especially exquisite.

Stainless-steel doors and hardware, made popular by their ability to withstand constant wear and tear with minimal maintenance, became common catalog items by the early 1930s. In addition to its use in custom designs commissioned by banks and civic buildings, stainless steel in the 1940s and 1950s became associated with the vernacular architecture of the roadside diner. Here the stamped metal's shininess gave interiors a spotless, sanitary aura coupled with a sleek modern look to create an icon of American design.

ALUMINUM

The first architectural use of aluminum in the United States took place on December 20, 1884, when a tiny pure aluminum pyramidal cap, approximately 12 inches tall and weighing 100 ounces, was set in place with great ceremony on top of the Washington Monument. At the time, aluminum was

considered a precious metal, and the cap for the monument was proudly displayed in Tiffany's window in New York prior to its installation. Although aluminum was still five times as expensive as copper in 1895, it had nonetheless secured a place for itself by then as an ornamental metal for architectural purposes. By the end of the century, stairs, elevators, and grilles were among the various items being cast in aluminum.

Thanks to a decline in price over the early years of the twentieth century, the use of aluminum as a decorative material steadily increased. With the Art Deco movement, its place with the other white metals, considered more "modern" than yellow metals such as brass and bronze, was ensured, and it became a favorite metal for decorative purposes, especially for interior trim in public and commercial buildings. Aluminum was relatively lightweight while being almost as strong and corrosion-resistant as stainless steel. It could be cast, extruded, rolled, hammered, or plated and was used extensively for ventilator grilles, stair railings, directory cases, elevator doors, and, especially, light fixtures, both interior and exterior. The architects of the Empire State Building, completed in 1931, made generous use of aluminum: the tower portion of the building, made famous by *King Kong,* is aluminum, as are the entrances, window spandrels, elevator doors, and other ornamental trim.

Made from copper and brass-plated cast iron, with a wooden capping on the railing, this balcony overlooked the main ballroom in the Elks Club National Headquarters on West Forty-third Street in New York City. The club was converted into the Diplomat Hotel, which was eventually demolished as part of the redevelopment of Times Square. The railing itself weighs over 100 pounds. Used here as a fireplace fender, it sits on its own, requiring no special installation.

NICKEL

Although most of us associate nickel with the five-cent piece of that name, the metal has been widely used in architectural ornament, in plating other metals, and, even more extensively, as a component of three alloys—nickel silver, Monel Metal, and stainless steel. Similar to iron in strength, it is comparable to copper in oxidation and resistance to corrosion.

From the 1870s through the 1930s, the technique of electroplating metals such as cast iron or brass with nickel was used to impart a silvery white color to such diverse architectural decoration as stair railings, grilles, signs, and hardware. Plating

Over the years the nickel plating on this Art Deco panel has worn away to reveal the warm yellow brass underneath. The intricate, stylized plant motifs in an Egyptian style were acid-etched into the brass prior to the plating, so they have not been affected by the loss of the nickel, and the piece retains all of its beauty. Originally one of three panels that graced the lobby of a federal building in Cleveland, this one has been cleverly incorporated into a Frank Lloyd Wright–inspired home. A horizontal molding of redwood running the length of the panel is anchored into the brick wall. The molding has a continuous groove that receives the panel; the bottom molding supports the weight, and an inverted top molding holds the panel against the wall. The existing custom redwood lighting fixtures at either end of the panel serve as the end pieces of the frame.

was often done in order to highlight certain ornament and to contrast it with the yellow or brown metals used elsewhere in a building. It was also used to plate plumbing fixtures, giving them a highly polished white finish.

Nickel silver was an especially popular material for architectural ornament in the Art Deco period. Also known as white brass, white bronze, or nickel bronze, this alloy generally contains 75 percent copper, 20 percent nickel, and 5 percent zinc, although the proportions can vary; it can be cast, rolled, extruded, pressed, hammered, or etched. By varying the percentage of metals, the manufacturer can modify the color, from silvery white to pale yellow, and the nickel silver can take on a pink, green, or blue cast as well. This play of colors and the metal's high polish appealed to designers during the first decades of the century, when a modern, machinelike look was highly valued; as a bonus, nickel silver has the practical quality of resisting corrosion. It was frequently used in conjunction with bronze to highlight important elements and to create a progression of decorative effects. An array of different-colored nickel silver ornament was sometimes used within the same building, often with stunning results, as can be seen in New York's legendary Waldorf-Astoria Hotel.

"Monel Metal" is a registered trademark for an alloy of nickel developed in 1905 whose properties and uses were precursors of stainless steel. Composed of approximately 66 percent nickel, 33 percent copper, and traces of iron, manganese, and silicon or carbon, it is similar in color to nickel and can be mirror-polished or left with a matte finish; the fabrication techniques are similar to those used for nickel silver except that Monel Metal cannot be extruded. Its first architectural use was as the roofing material for New York's Pennsylvania Station, where, from its installation in 1909 until

ELEVATOR LIGHTS WITH GRACEFUL DETAILING

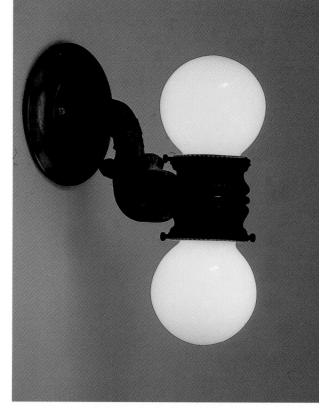

The lights on either side of this medicine cabinet started life as elevator indicators. When an elevator going up was approaching, the top light would glow; the bottom light would come on when the elevator was on its way down. The fixtures have been rewired so that both lights are illuminated at the same time. Made from cast iron and then copper-plated, they have a graceful form and lovely decorative detailing.

the building's demolition in 1965, it remained in excellent condition. As an ornamental metal, Monel Metal was particularly popular during the Art Deco era, along with the other white metals. The Union Trust Building in Detroit, built in 1928, featured over 40,000 pounds of Monel Metal in its clocks, grilles, gates, railings, signs, elevator doors, teller cages, desks, and screens, resulting in a stellar example of Art Deco architecture.

Nickel silver and Monel Metal were largely used in important buildings designed by well-known architects of the era. These materials had limited use in residential applications and were never available through catalogs. As a result, elements made from them were never as common as items made of iron, which was widely available and relatively inexpensive, or even bronze or brass, which had been in use much longer. It is therefore rare to find salvaged ornament made from nickel or Monel Metal.

Curiosity can lead to a wonderful treasure, as in the case of these beautiful wrought-iron light fixtures. When leaving an elegant restaurant on New York's Central Park South, the soon-to-be owner of these lights saw a Dumpster in front of the Essex House Hotel, which was under renovation at the time. Despite being in his good clothing, he climbed up the side of the Dumpster and peered in. What he found was a number of lighting fixtures covered with someone's leftover spaghetti dinner. Not having the slightest idea what he would do with the fixture, he proceeded to haul one out and take it home in a cab. When he got home he realized that he didn't have to hang the fixture from the ceiling, as it had originally been hung, but could rest it in this tri-part bay window. He quickly made two more trips to salvage a total of three fixtures. He placed lights within each fixture on the window ledge that cast a beautiful glow out through the opalescent glass and upward onto the ceiling above.

LIGHT FIXTURE FROM A POWER PLANT

A fragment of a cast-iron column, left, has been ingeniously reused as the base of a dictionary stand. The angled wooden support for the book is attached to a wooden post slightly smaller in diameter than the interior of the cast-iron column in which it rests. Sunny the cat guards this treasure.

An ornate cast-iron light fixture, above, was one of a series of entrance lights from a power plant in Richmond, Virginia, built in the early twentieth century. Originally they were painted silver. For their current use in a Manhattan office they have been sandblasted clean and then primed.

A lovely cast-iron ornament, right, sits atop a doorway, defining the opening and giving it visual interest.

During the renovation of an apartment, left, the contractor suggested moving the radiator in the dining area into an open space behind the wall. In order to cover the radiator he assembled five bronze pool scuppers on either side of the opening. He drilled holes into the returns on the scuppers and passed two threaded rods through them, one on the top, one on the bottom, to hold them in place. The scuppers were originally plated in nickel, to prevent corrosion in the wet pool environment. Over time the nickel wore off, exposing the bronze underneath, which oxidized into this attractive green patina.

Another use for the same pool scuppers can be seen at right, where the pretty pattern adds interest to the table. Any small metal grille can make an excellent trivet. Rubber or felt feet glued to the underside of the grille insulate the table from the heat and prevent it from being scratched.

When Dana Nicholson designed his space, he began buying odds and ends with a water and fire motif. One of the first things he found, in a junk store in Maine, was a mid-nineteenth-century cast-iron fireplace surround, which he turned into a decorative enclosure for a closet. His next purchase was an old metal bas-relief of Vulcan making lightning, which came from an English fireplace mantel. He hinged this bas-relief to the counter surface behind the closet doors so that it sits up when the doors are closed but lies flat when the doors are open. The door hardware was among the items salvaged from an Art Nouveau mansion in Scotland that had burned; these pieces were from the doors to a lady's dressing room.

In the 1800s cast-iron stars were commonly used as ornamental beam ties, holding the beams to the building's facade so that the masonry did not bow out over time. Stars of different sizes and styles can often be found as salvage. One of the simplest uses of these pieces is as candleholders—singly with a large candle or in pairs with delicate tapers. With simple alterations, which can be made by an ornamental iron worker, salvaged cast-iron star beam ties can find other uses. A flat plate can be tack welded to the bottom points of two small stars to transform them into bookends, or two large stars can have I-shaped supports attached perpendicularly to their backs to create a pair of andirons.

Darwin the cat surveys his domain, above, which includes a beautiful headboard made from three sections of a cast-bronze railing. The center panel is larger than the two outside panels and serves as a focal point. A continuous angle iron attached to the wall below the panels holds their weight, and polished bronze screws hold the panels against the wall. These highly ornate railings came from a movie theater that was demolished.

Metal grilles are particularly well suited to making an opening secure, since they are difficult to penetrate, yet allow light and air to pass through. Salvaged grilles can also make the opening a decorative element, as seen here, left. A cast-iron fish-scale grille, so called because the pattern resembles the scales of a fish, adds a distinctive look to a modern bathroom while making the window to a courtyard secure. This grille was one of 125 elevator transoms removed from the former New York Life Insurance Company building in Manhattan, along with 100 elevator doors. When laws requiring enclosed elevator shafts were enacted, the grilles were covered over with tin. Then in the early 1990s, when the elevators were modernized to become self-service, all of the grillework was removed.

A lovely wrought-iron door, left, originally found on an 1870s Brooklyn
brownstone, has been reused to secure
a window leading to a fire escape.
The width of the grille was perfect for
the space but it was too tall. The
grille was therefore cut at the bottom,
leaving intact the curved decorative
elements at the top while maintaining
the grille's structural integrity.

Hanging on the rear outer wall of
a town house, right, this section of
a wrought-iron stair railing softens the
rectilinear lines of the brick and the
doorway while also serving as a support for flowerpots. The same piece,
hung horizontally, would serve equally
well in a kitchen to hold pots and
pans, braids of garlic and peppers, and
bunches of herbs drying for the winter.

At home among an impressive display of antique metal folk art, left, which includes weather vanes and tools, are four recovered architectural pieces: a cast-iron star beam tie, a woman's head, a lion's face, and a number plaque. In the not-so-distant past, all of the items proudly displayed here would have been relegated to the trash. Luckily, they are now appreciated as examples of anonymous art.

The bedroom area of a studio apartment, right, is partitioned off with a wrought-iron Art Deco grille secured to the floor. The grille is one of a pair that came from the Beverly Wilshire Hotel in Los Angeles. Metal panels from grilles, doors, or fences make excellent room dividers, providing a sense of separation without closing off a space completely. If more privacy is desired, fabric can be put behind one face of the panel.

Metal grilles can be made into wonderful tabletops, as seen in this fine example, left, sitting on a screened porch. Painted steel legs have been welded to the underside of a large square cast-iron floor register from a barn in Bucks County, Pennsylvania. A glass top provides a smooth surface but allows the grille to be seen; a rabbeted redwood frame encloses and protects the glass. The table is particularly beautiful in this setting when sunlight passing through the ornate grille creates a delicate shadow on the floor.

A prized possession, a balustrade from the stairway of the Chicago Stock Exchange by Adler and Sullivan, sits in the study of a Prairie-style home, right. The balustrade has identical decoration on both sides and is perfectly symmetrical except for the angle on the very top where it was originally attached to the stair railing. In order to support the piece safely without attaching any-thing to it, small pins were anchored into the brick wall; the balustrade rests on the pins.

Opened in 1894, expanded in 1902, and demolished in 1988, the Corn Exchange
Building in lower Manhattan was considered an unusually modern-looking building
for its era. Stone angels and eagles on the corners were complemented by a cornice
composed of a series of copper lion heads, one of which is seen at left. Weighing only
about 4 pounds, the lion is simply hung on a picture hanger attached to the wall, using
a wire that was crimped to either side of the lion's mouth from behind.

Once part of an enormous fountain made by the J. W. Fiske foundry, this satyr,
above, playfully pours water into an indoor pool. Made of cast iron, it was one of four
that originally sat around the rim of the fountain's bowl.

Spanish-looking wrought-iron grilles, left, have been used to dress up a pair of closet doors. They are backed with opaque milk glass to hide the closet contents and to set off the pattern of the grilles. The motif of the wrought iron complements the southwestern style of the room's bench, textiles, and tribal headdresses.

The modern lines of a small bar in the Inn at Irving Place in Manhattan, right, are tempered by two antique lights. The ceiling fixture was originally made to hang tight up to the ceiling; the chains and canopy were added to allow light to project upward as well as through the opalescent glass panes. The wall fixture was not a light fixture at all, but rather an elevator indicator. It originally had two globes, one on top, one on the bottom, to indicate the direction of an arriving elevator. The globes were removed, the fixture rewired to accommodate one light, and a fluted shade was added. The copper plating of this cast-iron fixture echoes the copper counter of the wet bar.

A unique cast-iron railing from the Police Gazette Building in New York City is seen here set into a simple modern balcony. A shallow niche in the wall of the balcony frames the railing and allows a striking shadow to be cast. Another section of the same railing is on permanent display in the Frieda Schiff Warburg Sculpture Garden at the Brooklyn Museum.

In the course of redesigning and furnishing this home's interior, designer Terri McRay searched in vain for an appropriate fire screen. Instead, she fell in love with an ornate polished brass grille from a mansion in Maine. The grille became the centerpiece for this custom-made screen, which she designed. Hammered polished brass pieces with stencil-cut decorations were added to the grille's top and bottom and as side returns. The screen reflects light from the fire, adding a jewel-like quality to the room.

To create an elegant kitchen door, four register grilles from a school-house in Rhode Island were combined and set into two teak frames. The frames were then joined with piano hinges to make a bifold door that hangs on a track screwed into the ceiling. One side of the door was hung with fabric to screen the kitchen and also to hide the backs of the grilles, which are flat and therefore not decorative.

NEW USES FOR PANELS, GRILLES, AND DOORS

When coming up with new uses for metal panels, such as grilles, doors, or fencing, it is important to remember their general characteristics. Panels tend to be fairly two-dimensional, although some have more depth than others. They allow the passage of light and air, and they tend to be strong and rigid. The shadows they cast can be extremely beautiful and will add interest to any space. Made from almost every metal in every finish and in every style imaginable, they can easily be reused in a wide variety of settings. They also range in size from small registers to hundred-foot-long railings. Most metal panels are rectilinear, although it is not unusual to find them with one curved edge or in half or even full circles. Multiple small panels can be grouped together in a frame to accomplish the same effect as a single large panel.

LIGHT FIXTURES

Small metal grilles can make wonderful light fixtures. Individually or in pairs they can become lovely wall sconces; in sets of three or more they can be joined together to make a long fixture or a soffit to hide a light. To build a sconce, set the grille into a wood or metal frame and place a frosted-glass or acrylic diffuser panel behind it. If you want to illuminate only the face of the sconce, make returns on all sides that match the frame and completely enclose the fixture. If you leave off the top and bottom return but retain the sides, the sconce can wash the wall above and below with light. If you pin the sconce off the wall but make a return just wide enough to obscure the lightbulbs from the sides, you can wash the wall all around with light.

A folding screen created from three matching metal grilles also can provide a sense of separation. Privacy can be enhanced by hanging fabric behind the grille to totally obscure what lies beyond the screen. Depending on the weight of the panels and how often they will be moved, they can be joined with continuous piano hinges or with simple hooks and eyes.

FOLDING SCREEN

MAGAZINE RACK

You can use a pair of metal grilles to create an unusual magazine rack. Weld a steel plate or bar to the bottom edges or the inside faces of the grilles to hold them together. Then fix a wooden base to the steel elements to hold the entire structure off the floor and to prevent the magazines from falling down.

HEADBOARD

You can make a beautiful headboard by attaching metal panels to a wall, as shown on pages 54 and 75. Or you can attach two matching panels directly to a bed frame, one at the head, the other at the foot. The footboard should, of course, be set lower.

SPACE DIVIDER

Large metal panels or doors can be used effectively to separate spaces without completely enclosing them. For example, a home office or work space is often set up within a larger room. Setting the desk between a pair of metal grilles backed with fabric or frosted-glass panels will define the space, hide the clutter, and give the impression of separation without isolating the area completely. The grille will also allow air and light to filter in, minimizing any claustrophobia.

BEIDL

INS

STONE &
TERRA COTTA

STONE HAS ALWAYS BEEN ASSOCIATED WITH MONUMENTALITY: THE PYRAMIDS

of Egypt, the temple complex at Angkor Wat, the fortifications and cathedrals of

Europe, and the grand civic structures of the nineteenth century were all constructed

of stone. Just as the history of countless civilizations has been recorded on stone, so

too has it been used for grave markers to record personal histories. To be "written

in stone" signifies something that will not change over time. It is therefore doubly

sad that wonderful masonry buildings built to stand for centuries time and again

have been relentlessly demolished without a second thought.

    According to Barbara Millstein, curator of the Frieda Schiff Warburg Sculpture

Garden at the Brooklyn Museum, the story of stone ornament in the United States

is that of the itinerant stone carvers, most of them immigrants, who traveled the rails and carried their tools with them from city to city. Adolescent boys who had been trained in a stone yard in Europe were often sent by their families to live with a relative in the New World who could get them a job carving in an American stone yard. The first Europeans to come to the United States as carvers were English; they were soon followed by Germans and by emancipated slaves who migrated to the North. Each ensuing wave of immigration brought carvers of a new nationality: the Irish, the Italians, especially those from the areas near the great quarries, and finally the Eastern Europeans.

Boys would live with an uncle or another family member, and immediately begin to earn their livelihood as stone carvers. It was often a lonely life, but they did have a freedom to express themselves in stone that did not exist at home. In Europe, stone carvers worked within an established tradition of form and content, usually joining their fathers and uncles in the trade and living and working near the job site. In addition, certain groups—Jews, for instance—were not allowed to work as carvers in Europe. But in the United States they could carve, and they carved ebulliently.

There were no rules limiting the kind of designs that could be attempted and often little direction from architects and builders. These artisans creatively

Previous page: Detail of the demolished American Life Insurance Building in Philadelphia.

These large terra-cotta frieze blocks, opposite, from a Harlem tenement building have been adapted to serve as unusual table bases. To create each support, two blocks were cemented back to back so that they would be attractive seen from either direction. (The blocks, when set into the original building, were, of course, one-sided.) Limestone plinths were fabricated for the base and the top of each support, and a glass tabletop was then set in place.

adapted traditional designs from Europe, incorporating the faces of people they knew or images from their own vivid imaginations into the framework of classical ornament. Style books were in use, of course. Franz Sales Meyers's *Handbook of Ornament* and *The Style of Ornament* by Alexander Speltz were two of the best known and most popular. These books depicted the panoply of traditional designs that had been incorporated into building ornament from Babylonian and Assyrian times right up until the middle of the nineteenth century.

American stone carvers simply chose elements they fancied and then combined them with abandon, mating Asian ornament with Greek ornament, perhaps, or Roman ornament with Egyptian ornament. A row of palmettos with an egg-and-dart border might share space on a frieze with acanthus leaves. The face on a keystone might be that of the carver's sweetheart, and a dragon gargoyle might have the face of the family dog. And it was this extraordinary fusion of ornamentation that made architectural carving in America so unique.

Stone carving was a difficult trade. The carvers traveled from city to city to find work. Their hours were long, and almost all of them became afflicted with silicosis, which was called "old stone cutters' disease." As a result, they rarely made it past the age of thirty-five or forty. Between 1840 and 1880, very few stone carvers even bothered to marry: they were constantly on the move, and they feared leaving behind a widow and family. But they nonetheless took on the status of folk heroes, and many of them were known by their style and appreciated for their work.

Every little stone yard had one or two carvers. The rest of the workers were stonecutters who prepared quarried stone into blocks for the building's facade or for the carved ornament. Perhaps because of their artistic temperament, the stone carvers were never able to organize themselves into a union.

*When the Newark, New Jersey, Post
Office was demolished in the 1930s, the
grandfather of the current owner of
this garden decided to salvage a portion
of the ornament from the building.
Plaques, friezes, column and pilaster
capitals, corbels, and finials were
all combined to create fanciful walls,
stairs, and an enclosure for a
fountain rescued from another site.
The delicacy of the ornamental
detail contrasts beautifully with the
rough-hewn quality of the stone
in which it is set.*

Stonecutters, on the other hand, had a very strong union, and so by the end of the nineteenth century, the well-organized cutters were earning more than the stone carvers.

In the first part of the nineteenth century an owner putting up a large building would hire carvers from the stone yards that produced the specific stone needed. The developer or the architect would then request a certain number of Johns (a John was the face of a young man) or Moseses (the faces of bearded men) or Marys (women's faces) and perhaps some angels or cherubs. What the faces would actually look like was rarely specified but was left up to the sculptor. If more than one stone carver worked on a building, the faces would not be uniform, and on a large building, where many carvers might be working, there could be a dizzying assortment of styles.

This visual cacophony went on unchecked until a few enterprising carvers at the end of the nineteenth century set up studios independent of the stone yards. One of the best known of these was founded by a man named John Donnelly, who established a carving dynasty in which all of the male members of his family carved. Donnelly, who had come to the United States when he was twelve or thirteen years old, recognized the need for architects and owners to be able to determine the style of carvings prior to their execution. So he opened a little studio where plaster casts could be made to exact dimensions and specifications, and only upon their approval would the carvers be engaged to execute these designs to order. Responsible for the magnificent sculpture on New York's Grand Central Station and on the main branch of the New York Public Library, Donnelly's company was still carving when Rockefeller Center went up in the 1930s.

The carvers didn't just work on elaborate civic structures, fancy stores, and grand mansions. They also carved ornament for the tenements that were going up to house each new wave of immigrants. Lintels, keystones, and pediments were carved to make these tenements look more attractive—and to camouflage what lay inside. Jacob Riis relates the following in *How the Other Half Lives,* his description of tenement life in New York: "Here, as we stroll along Madison Street, workmen are busy putting the finishing touches to the brownstone front of a tall new tenement. . . . They are carving satyrs' heads in the stone, with a crowd of gaping youngsters looking on in admiring wonder. . . . Is it only in our fancy that the sardonic leer on the stone faces seems to list that way? Or is it an introspective grin?" Perhaps only the stone carver knew for sure.

GRANITE

The hardest and most difficult to carve of all the stones, granite has usually been reserved for the most important and expensive buildings. It is an igneous rock, created when a molten mass from deep within the earth cools as it moves toward the earth's surface; the rate of cooling determines the degree of crystallization and the final composition of the rock. In the case of granite, the material cools very slowly, well below the earth's surface, and is as a result completely crystalline and coarse-grained. Granite is composed largely of silica, most commonly in combination with small amounts of feldspar and mica. It can vary in color from black to white, with many shades in between, and is often mottled with red or pink.

Granite was first exploited in the United States simply because of its availability, not its ease of use. It made its earliest appearances in grave markers and stair treads. As it became increasingly routine in the nineteenth century for unscrupulous politicians to award building and material contracts

For over forty years, from the mid-1800s almost to the end of the century, brownstone was the preferred facing and carving material for row houses in New York City and many other urban areas. This plaque from a town house, with its fanciful carved griffin, is set into a brick wall adjacent to a driveway. The weight is carried by the brick base, and the sides are held in place by the brick walls that were built to overlap the plaque by about an inch both in front and in back.

to their friends and relatives, the type of stone used in a building often depended as much on whose relative owned a particular quarry as it did on the availability and accessibility of the material, the color, and the characteristics of the stone.

Granite was often used on facades as well as interiors because of its strength and weather resistance. It could be quarried in long lengths and transported without breaking, making it a popular choice for columns and for long architectural friezes. To carve granite required special tools and techniques, largely because of its hardness, but the durability of the stone often outweighed the inconvenience and cost of carving it. Salvaged granite ornament is not very common today, although it can occasionally be found as plaques, stair railings, balusters, columns, or friezes.

SANDSTONE

From the 1840s to the early 1900s, sandstone was one of the most widely used building materials in the United States. Commonly known as brownstone, this material could vary in color from a warm brown to a rich red to a deep pink and even to cream, depending on its mineral content, but it was the earth-toned color range that became popular in American cities. In contrast to marble and granite, sandstone was easy to quarry, to cut, and

Ornament does not necessarily have to be used in the same direction as it was on the original building. The elements that appear to be columns supporting the glass tabletop in this picture are actually segments of terra-cotta banding that once ran horizontally across a building. Standing on end, they serve wonderfully as supports. On the table is a sandstone column capital from the old New Haven, Connecticut, City Hall. Turned upside down, it now supports a Bacchus face, grinning up rather than looking down from the top of a building.

to carve, making it relatively economical as well as attractive. Entire neighborhoods were built from brownstone, especially the row houses that dominated cities after the Civil War. As tastes changed toward the end of the nineteenth century, limestone, which is off-white or gray, took over from sandstone as the dominant building stone.

The characteristics that make sandstone easy to work are also responsible for its reputation as a troublesome material. It is a sedimentary rock, formed near the surface of the earth when rock particles, or sediment, are deposited in an area. This sediment is then bound together, either through pressure or with the introduction of a binding material such as clay or silica. Over time, more and more layers of sediment are bound together in a process called stratification. Because of this stratification, all sedimentary stone sits in distinct layers known as bedding planes. When a block of sandstone is brought up out of the quarry, it must immediately be marked to indicate which side is the face plane and which is the bedding plane. (This was usually done at a nearby bench, hence the word "benchmark.")

If sandstone is carved on the side that is easiest to carve, its vertical face, the layers of the stone will eventually peel apart like the pages of a book. If carved on the horizontal face, sandstone will last almost indefinitely—but this is much harder to do. Unscrupulous developers, in their desire to speed construction and reduce costs, did not always pay careful attention to the benchmark. This situation was aggravated when old buildings were torn down and the stone was reused as a facing material or for carved ornament. Sometimes the benchmark was no longer visible; other times it was conveniently ignored. As a result, sandstone has acquired an undeserved reputation as a material that does not stand up over time.

LIMESTONE

Limestone is a sedimentary stone composed principally of calcite and dolomite. These two elements are cemented together over long periods of time by calcium carbonate from the shells and skeletons of marine organisms in solution. Trace minerals, such as carbonates and oxides of iron, silica, mica, and talc, give limestone a wide range of colors and density. Eastern limestone tends to be softer than the limestone from the Midwest. Indiana limestone, for example, can be as hard and dense as marble, although even within Indiana limestone there are significant differences in density and hue.

Limestone has been one of the most popular building stones throughout history. The pyramids of Egypt were built of massive blocks of limestone, the Assyrians created beautiful reliefs in limestone, and the Greeks and Romans used it for much of their architecture. The best limestone can be carved with intricate detail and polished like marble. The softer limestone can, however, be as vulnerable to weathering as sandstone, especially if it is not laid with the grain running as it does in the quarry.

In the United States, limestone was regularly used for facades, but the peak of its popularity coincided with the era of exuberant architectural ornamentation from the 1880s to the 1920s. Prior to that time, sandstone was the dominant building material in most urban areas. But when styles at the end of the 1800s turned from the darker earth-toned materials to lighter ones, limestone, along with terra cotta, became the premier material for creating ornament. Keystones, door and window surrounds, archways, friezes, brackets, corbels, and balconies were routinely carved from limestone and are commonly found as salvage today.

MARBLE

Marble is a noble material, one that has traditionally been used for sculpture. Its general lack of a distinctive grain makes it particularly suitable for carving, and its relatively fine texture means the piece can be brought to a highly polished finish. These traits have made marble one of the preferred materials for statuary on major buildings.

Marble is actually limestone that has been heated by adjacent molten rock. It is composed, like limestone, mostly of calcite, but other minerals added during metamorphosis, such as mica, silica, graphite, or iron oxides, give marble a wide range of colors, from almost pure white through the pinks to red and to green, usually intermingled with gray or black. White marbles became especially popular for facing buildings after the World's Columbian Exposition of 1893, which had required that all its major buildings be designed in a Beaux Arts style and painted white to evoke the classical spirit of Greece and Rome; this led to a general shift in architecture from dark to light materials.

Marble as salvage comes more often from interiors than from building exteriors. Floors, walls, ornamental detail, and in particular, fireplace mantels were very often fabricated from marble, since its wide variety of colors and markings, coupled with its ability to be carved and polished, made it very popular.

These carved limestone pilasters sat on either side of the entrance to a Harlem apartment house. They have been turned sideways to form the doorway of a corporate conference room. The entrance is capped off with the keystone from an apartment house in Brooklyn that burned and was subsequently demolished. The lovely woman's demure face was cast in off-white terra cotta.

CAST STONE

Similar in nature to concrete, cast stone became popular after the turn of the century as a material for architectural ornament, especially in the southern states. It often weathers better than real stone, and is particularly well suited to ornamental uses because it can hold fine details in casting, details that would be prohibitively expensive to produce by hand carving. Like terra cotta, it afforded great savings where repetitive ornament or patterns were desired.

Through the use of various aggregates that were added to the basic mixture of Portland cement, sand, and water, color and finish could be altered to achieve a desired effect; limestone or brownstone, for example, could easily be imitated by adding pigments. During the Art Deco era, nonfading limeproof pigments allowed cast stone to be used extensively to create decorative patterns on building facades. Stone chips would also be added to the mix and then polished when the stone hardened to give different effects, with mica, in particular, often added to give a brilliance to the finished ornament. Salvage items commonly found in cast stone are garden ornaments, fountains, and repetitive decorative elements such as friezes and banding.

TERRA COTTA

Terra cotta, Italian for "cooked earth," is one of the oldest building materials known to civilization. Like brick, it is made from clay, but is more compact than brick and fired at a higher temperature, producing a material that is generally harder. Most often used for cladding buildings or creating ornamentation, architectural terra cotta is one of the most prevalent masonry building materials in our urban environment. Clay with the desired pliability, density, or color is used to make decorative hollow blocks, either by casting or occasionally by hand molding. The blocks contain internal stiffeners and

It is sometimes difficult to find a mantel that fits a fireplace exactly and also suits your tastes. In this case, designer Zohreh Zand used individual pieces of terra cotta to create a custom mantel at a fraction of the cost of a comparable stone fireplace. The mantel is made from a nineteenth-century terra-cotta window pediment; the large central piece sat above a window, and the two side pieces were corbels supporting it on either side of the window. The custom-made shelf above the plaque is limestone. All of the elements are cemented to the wall with mortar.

are most often, but not always, much larger than individual bricks, requiring two hands to set in place.

Many ancient cultures have left us baked clay artifacts to record their passing. The Romans, in particular, used clay to protect wood and stone from the weather as well as to create decorative elements that might otherwise have been made in stone. With the fall of the Roman Empire, the use of terra cotta declined in Europe until its revival during the Renaissance. In the Italy of the fourteenth and fifteenth centuries, it was used extensively to decorate palaces and cathedrals, and the town of Faenza was so renowned for its superior work that especially fine terra cotta became known as faience. Spain, where the Moors had reintroduced terra-cotta molding and glazing techniques, also produced beautiful ornamentation. Terra cotta became popular in England during the Tudor period, especially for

manor homes, although it fell out of favor during the Reformation, when trade with Italy, where the best clays came from, was greatly reduced. The English terra-cotta industry grew into its own during the late 1700s and early 1800s and served the limited needs of the United States as well.

In 1840 the United States had its first terra-cotta factory with the opening of the Worcester Works in Massachusetts. The material produced there was rarely recognizable as terra cotta, however, because it was painted to resemble metal or stone, depending on its use and the owner's preference. In other cities, builders who wanted to use terra cotta were often forced to order the material from pottery makers, sewer-pipe factories, or other clay-working companies who were unfamiliar with the requirements of architectural terra cotta. This led to numerous construction failures and a subsequent distrust of the material, one that was encouraged by stonecutters who feared for their livelihood.

Terra cotta got its greatest boost from the devastating fire of 1871 in Chicago. After inspecting the destruction, architects and builders realized that the structural members and facades of the surviving buildings were, in many instances, insulated with terra cotta or brick. Upon reflection this makes absolute sense: terra cotta is exposed to temperatures exceeding 2000° F. during the firing process and can therefore withstand temperatures that would destroy or deform other materials. The rebuilding of Chicago, coupled with the 1870 opening of the Chicago Terra Cotta Company, whose kilns and experienced craftsmen were imported from England, made that city, and in turn the Midwest, the center for terra cotta over the next decade.

Terra cotta, along with cast iron, was a material well suited to an era when traditional handcrafts were being replaced by mechanized production. Buildings in the late 1800s and early 1900s were designed with repetitive decorative elements; to cut them in stone by hand would have been extremely costly. By adapting designs to be mass-produced in clay, considerable cost savings could be realized without aesthetic compromises: once a mold was made, many pieces could be cast from it, amortizing the initial cost, and these designs, like those in cast iron, could be sold through catalogs.

Although it was an industrialized product, many of the actual processes involved in the production of terra cotta were done by hand. Highly skilled sculptors created clay patterns from which plaster and, later, rubber molds were made. Clay was pressed by hand into the molds and remained there to stiffen and shrink slightly, allowing for easy removal from the mold. These clay blocks were finished by workers who smoothed them, removed the

Stone capitals make splendid bases for glass-topped tables. At Crocodile Studio, a New York City art gallery, both a conference table (which could just as easily be a dining table) and a console table were constructed from a series of terra-cotta pilaster capitals, each featuring a pair of frolicking dolphins. Because pilaster capitals are set into the building's facade rather than being freestanding like column capitals, they are one-sided. Building the console table, which sits against a wall and is therefore also one-sided, was straightforward. A single capital was placed on a limestone shaft cut to fit; the original pilaster shafts for these capitals were brick and therefore not salvaged. The terra-cotta base of the pilaster was then cemented to the new shaft. The dining table support was created by cementing back-to-back two identical bases.

seam marks, and in some cases incorporated additional carving; the blocks were then dried.

The earliest type of terra cotta, often referred to as brownstone terra cotta, was left unglazed or was given a slip glaze. Later types of terra cotta received a white or colored glaze. After glazing, the blocks were fired in special kilns at temperatures ranging from 2100° up to 2500° F. for eight to fourteen days. The blocks then received additional finishing to ensure a proper fit when laid into place and were numbered and keyed to a plan for their installation. The decoration on some terra-cotta stones was, however, entirely hand-finished, with stonecutters entering the terra-cotta industry to produce magnificent carvings that rivaled the work done in stone.

Because it is a fraction of the weight of solid stone, the use of terra cotta reduced shipping and installation costs, while the structures supporting the material could be lighter, further reducing the cost of a building. The rise in popularity of terra cotta also coincided with the development of the elevator, allowing buildings to rise to unprecedented heights. The entire weight of these tall buildings, first called cloudscrapers and then skyscrapers, was carried by the structural steel frame rather than the walls. The outer enclosure of the building, which was not load-bearing, became known as a curtain wall, meaning that it formed a nonstructural curtain or enclosure. Using terra cotta to clad the structural frame became one of the most common practices

Because its owner is a longtime collector, Smith and Wollensky, one of the best-known restaurants in New York, features numerous examples of architectural ornament in its dining areas. Superb examples of the craft, these terra-cotta pieces were beautifully integrated into the dining room walls. Often the sides of terra cotta are not attractive since they were never intended to be seen, but when the pieces are set into the wall, almost flush with it, the sides are completely hidden. These images seem to cast a benign eye on the tables, wishing the diners "Bon appétit!"

As seen above, the patterns on many small terra-cotta blocks have a strong central motif, creating an ideal place to set a candle. No matter how low the candle burns, the terra cotta will withstand the heat and protect the surface it sits upon.

These two pieces of carved limestone, left, formed the decorative end caps of a horizontal band on a masonry facade. Unlike many facade elements they have carving on two sides, not just on the part that faced out from the building, so they make great bookends, interesting from the front and the side. The only preparation required was to chip off the excess mortar that remained after their removal and put some felt on the bottom to protect the surface on which they rest.

This keystone and arch in the
form of a winged and plumed
cartouche originally surrounded
one of the windows in a
Harlem tenement building.
Cast in off-white terra cotta, it
dates from the end of the
nineteenth century. The arch
now embraces the dividers
between sets of filing cabinets
in the conference room of a
New York marketing firm.

Decorative chimney pots were used to cover air vents and provide a graceful finish to a chimney. They can sometimes be found in salvage yards and antiques stores in a wide variety of sizes, shapes, and styles, and the uses they can be put to are myriad, limited only by imagination. At left, a decorative glazed terra-cotta chimney pot from England found a new use as an umbrella stand.

Because they were fabricated to be used on rooftops, terra-cotta chimney pots are particularly well suited for outdoor use. A lovely garden lamp, left, has been made out of a chimney pot from a London row house. The vents were designed to increase the draft and now allow light to spill out of the sides as well as from the opening at the top. A different style of chimney pot is shown on a summer porch, right, functioning as an oversize vase holding tall stalks of ornamental grass.

Preceding page: Black cats bring good luck when they come from the Palisades Amusement Park. The cartoonlike style of these two cats was appropriate for the fantasy atmosphere of the amusement park. Sitting over 8 feet tall and made out of cast stone, they now flank a residential driveway. The use of large decorative elements like these cats instantly creates a landmark and an identity, distinguishing this property from its neighbors. The owners have often emerged from their driveway to find passersby posing for photographs next to the cats. On holidays the cats get appropriately decorated—red, white, and blue garlands for the Fourth of July, for example, and twinkle lights for Christmas—but they stay just as they are for Halloween.

In 1995 sixty terra-cotta lion's heads were removed from the facade of the former Vanderbilt Hotel at 4 Park Avenue in New York City. Designed in 1912 by Warren and Wetmore, the same firm that designed Grand Central Station, the hotel was the height of elegance in its day, but it has since been converted to an office building. This rescued lion's head, above, has been reused to enclose the jet of a fountain in the garden of a Brooklyn town house. The lion's head did not originally have a hole to accommodate the spout, so one was created. Using a small masonry bit an initial hole was made. Increasingly larger bits were used until the desired diameter was achieved. Starting very small and gradually increasing the size of the bit helped prevent too much stress being placed on the terra cotta, which could crack and break the ornament.

Despite their weight, terra-cotta plaques can be hung on a wall as art. The motif of the plaque, left, echoes the spirit of the botanical prints on the adjacent wall. This plaque is typical of those that decorate many urban apartment buildings, including tenements.

Peeking out from the plants in this lush indoor garden, below, is a terra-cotta gargoyle that came from a school building in Brooklyn. Because this piece came from a facade, it would be equally at home in an outdoor garden.

TERRA-COTTA GARGOYLE

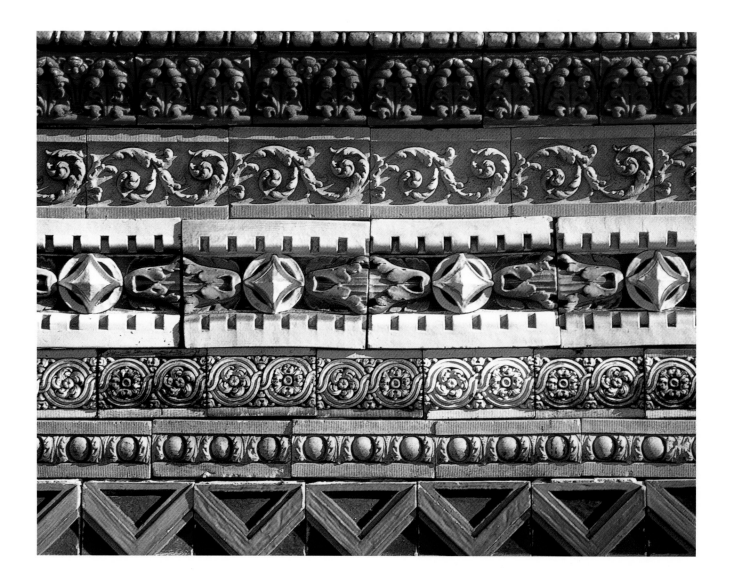

THE BEAUTY OF TERRA-COTTA BLOCKS

Terra-cotta blocks are incredibly versatile. They come in many decorative styles, from classical to Art Deco and, thanks to their glazing, in almost every color. Most often used in repetitive patterns, especially as banding, they are often available in sets. But even if you have only a pair, you can use the blocks as candleholders (page 121) or bookends (page 120) or set them in a garden or on a shelf as a purely decorative accent. The most interesting uses, however, take advantage of them in a series. Usually the only preparation needed is a good cleaning with a mild soap and water. Sometimes excess mortar needs to be removed so that they will sit evenly, but gently chipping off this old mortar with a chisel and hammer is a relatively simple task.

DROP-IN BATHTUB

Much like ceramic tile, terra cotta resists water and is easy to keep clean, making it a terrific material for reuse in bathrooms. As seen above, the blocks are used to create steps and a surround for a drop-in bathtub. The individual blocks are cemented together, and slabs of the same material used on the floor—perhaps granite, marble, or ceramic tile—are set over the blocks to make treads.

At left, blocks are used to create a vanity, forming the sides and supporting the sink and countertop. Above the vanity, the blocks are used to create a soffit with a light hidden behind it.

VANITY

POOL EDGING

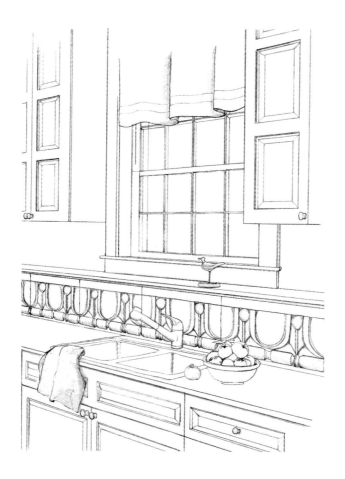

It is not unusual to come upon a very large number of identical terra-cotta tiles. In that case, a decorative fountain or fishpond or even a swimming pool would make wonderful use of the set. Above, the tiles are shown as an edging that is set just above the waterline of a pool.

The kitchen is also an ideal place in which to use terra-cotta blocks, since they resist heat, water, and food spills. To make a decorative backsplash, as seen at left, you can use a series of blocks the way you would use ceramic tile—set into mortar one block next to another. You can then top the blocks with a piece of the countertop material, creating a functional shelf.

BACKSPLASH

It is rare to find an Art Deco mantel, so why not create one using glazed architectural terra cotta, which was widely used during the Art Deco period. The blocks shown here are stacked four high to create a frame approximately 36 inches tall; the number of blocks used for the height and the width can vary depending on the size of the wall and the scale of the room. As pictured here, the blocks are set into the wall, leaving 1 inch exposed beyond the face of the wall to create a shallow frame. They could also be set in flush or allowed to jut farther out to make a deeper surround. Since the sides of the blocks are unfinished, a 1-inch-thick slab of marble or slate can be installed around the perimeter to cover the rough sides. The beauty of terra cotta for use as a mantel is that it can withstand heat, since it has already been fired at over 2000° F. It also offers interesting patterns not often found in fireplaces.

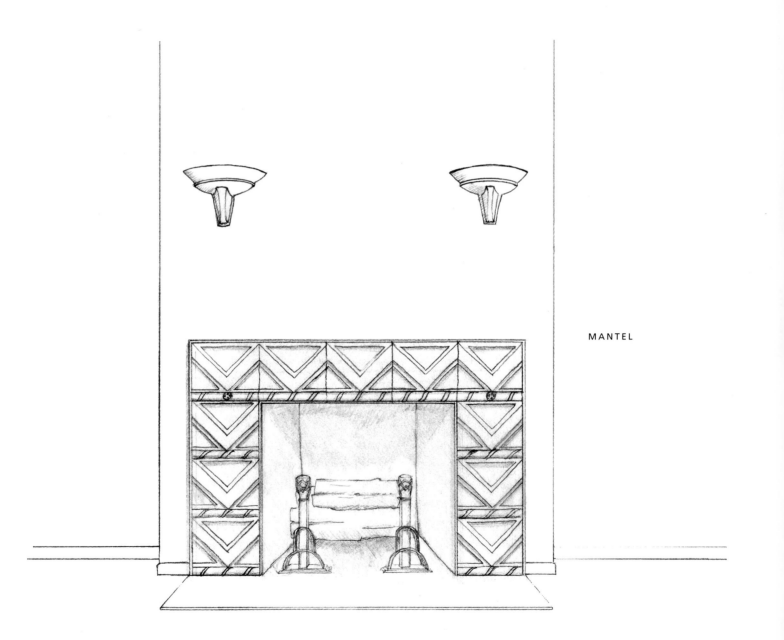

MANTEL

OUTDOOR BARBECUE

Because stone withstands heat very well, it can be used to create an impressive outdoor barbecue. If the structure of the barbecue is masonry, either brick or block, the task of supporting and securing the surround will be relatively simple. The capitals and the surround will rest on the masonry and can be cemented to the structure on the back. The keystone is also cemented to the structure, but you will need to provide a steel dowel to hold its weight until the cement sets.

Simultaneously practical and spectacular, a range hood hiding an exhaust fan over a stove can be created with a stone surround set flush with the overhead cabinets and attached to a structural frame. Given the weight of the surround and the variables of the surrounding structure, this frame should be designed by a professional. A baffle can fill in the space in the surround or it can be left open at the back. The beauty of this use of a surround is that it will be absolutely unaffected by the heat of cooking.

RANGE HOOD

Stone surrounds vary in depth, but most are 6 to 12 inches deep, making them ideal for reuse as frames for a china cabinet, a bar, or bookshelves. How the surround is to be held in place will depend on the wall structure behind it. If the wall is masonry, the sections of the surround can be cemented directly to the masonry with dowels to support them until the cement sets. If it is not masonry, you will need to reinforce the wall so that it will support the added weight.

CHINA CABINET

WOOD

WOOD HAS BEEN THE MOST UNIVERSAL AND USEFUL OF ALL BUILDING MATERIALS

throughout history. It can serve as structure, as enclosure, and as ornament. It can

be carved, sawed, incised, or turned on a lathe. Although few examples of ancient

wooden ornament of any sort have survived the ravages of time, the use of wood

has historically depended on the variety of trees available locally. In the early United

States, trees that were felled to make way for settlement and for cultivation were

immediately put to use in building nearby structures, and until the end of the nine-

teenth century, the use of wood continued to be regional. But as the population

grew, as local forests dwindled, and as the Far East was opened up to trade, wood

began to be transported over longer distances, and exotic woods from around the world were increasingly used, especially in the mansions built for the new class of industrial magnates.

Almost without exception, the wood used before the turn of the century is superior in strength and decay-resistance to wood currently available. Today's plantation-grown trees, which provide the bulk of the wood harvested in the United States, grow quickly and as a result have only three to five growth rings per inch of diameter. Old timber, which was harvested from mature trees that grew slowly in virgin forests, generally had twenty-five to thirty annual rings per inch. In addition, some species such as the American chestnut, which was used extensively in the northeastern United States, are virtually extinct.

With the development of iron and, later, steel framing, wood, by the end of the nineteenth century, was rarely used structurally for nonresidential buildings due to its flammability. At the same time, however, there was a boom in residential construction, which, combined with the era's love of embellishment, led to some of the most creative wood ornament ever made.

A truly indigenous form of wooden building ornament was developed in America by carpenters and joiners who finished houses with decorative elements that were created with saws rather than carved. Often based on Gothic motifs, these fanciful porch railings, shingles, and gables add visual delight to otherwise modest homes, both by their own forms and by the shadows they cast. Known as gingerbread, these details represent a charming intersection of Yankee thrift, since they were often sawed from scrap lumber, and the carpenters' desire to show off their skill.

The range of salvaged items made of wood is very wide. Exterior items such as porch railings, columns, corbels, cornices, doors, windows, and shutters are quite common, although they may need

Previous page: Detail of the south stairway in the residence at 212 East Court Street in Ithaca, New York.

This home doesn't have a fireplace, opposite, but that fact didn't deter the owner from purchasing a lovely carved wooden mantel. She simply leaned it up against the wall and then decorated it with interesting objects to create an attention-getting "stage set." She decided to leave the mantel in the state in which she found it, only partially stripped of its paint. The shapes of the beautiful carvings are easily discernible while the mottling of the old paint layers adds to the visual interest.

extensive restoration because of exposure to the elements. Interior elements such as doors, wainscoting and paneling, decorative flooring, moldings, ceilings, mantels, carved beams, brackets, columns, balusters, newel posts, and stair railings are often in good condition but may be covered with layers of paint. Finding a way to use these wooden elements is extremely rewarding.

The Inn at Irving Place is a unique bed-and-breakfast in New York City's elegant Gramercy Park neighborhood. Two town houses that had been in the owner's family were completely renovated and then joined to create the inn. There was little architectural detail remaining in the buildings prior to the renovation, so the owner and her architect decided to use old mantels and lighting fixtures to create the desired ambience. At right and below, a columned oak mantel with an overmantel mirror and a magnificent cast-iron summer front becomes the focal point of a sitting room. In a bedroom, left, the simple yet elegant mantel forms a counterpoint to the ornate bed frame and sumptuous linens.

When the owner of a very modern loft and his architect, J. P. Friedman, saw these massive carved black walnut doors, they fell in love with them and decided to use them as the entrance doors to the master bedroom. The doorway was created to fit the dimensions of the doors, and the frame was reinforced to hold their weight, which is significant because the doors are almost 10 feet tall. The contrast of the detailed and layered millwork of the dark wood against the simple lines and modern white surfaces of the adjacent areas is stunning and creates a strong focal point for this wing of the loft.

These unusual carved pine Italianate columns date from the first half of the nineteenth century. Originally, rectangular pieces above and below the capitals had attached them to a wall. These pieces were embellished with flowerets, giving designer Dana Nicholson the motif he reused on two sides of the new teak bases he created. He had the columns and flowerets finished in a parchment color and applied gold, blue, and a little purple to them to highlight the filigree. The owner had used four columns in her previous apartment. But in her current home, which has an open plan, she uses only three of them, moving them about the apartment to alter the feel of the spaces.

Previous page: The panel of a choir loft from a rural church was used to create a dramatic headboard. It is a wonderful example of the Gothic Revival style, popular during the Victorian years in the United States, with its hand-carved pointed arches and quatrefoils. After this piece was salvaged and refinished, each of the arches was padded with an upholstered panel of exactly the same shape, providing a comfortable backrest for reading in bed. The panel, which is solid oak, weighs about 75 pounds. Four heavy-duty storm sash hangers were used to attach it to the wall. The headboard can be removed when needed to give access to the electrical wiring behind.

Whether in their first home in a drugstore or in their current home in a kitchen, these glass-and-walnut cabinets, above, are immensely practical and lovely. They provide a great deal of storage and at the same time add a dimension to the kitchen that could not have been achieved with contemporary cabinets.

A lovely mirror, left, was fashioned from an early 1800s arched wooden door transom from a Philadelphia town house. The owner added the three pieces of the frame below the transom and then backed it up with a mirror. Since the old wood and the new wood didn't match, the entire piece was finished with red japan lacquer, creating a stunning and functional addition to this home.

In creating this room within a room in a renovated loft, the architect Barry Berg utilized two different pieces of architectural salvage: a set of porch panels and a dormer window. The panels came from the enclosed porch of a mansion in the Riverdale section of the Bronx once owned by the founder of the Bond Bread Company. One of the panels was fixed to either side of the front opening of the room to build a divider and a third one, between the other two, was hinged to create a door. They were faced with a lacy fabric to make the space more private. Having created this interior room without any windows for ventilation, Berg set a round dormer window, originally from a synagogue in New Jersey, into the ceiling. The window pivots to open or close, functioning as a vent. For additional interest, a spotlight with an M16 halogen bulb is directed from the floor up through the dormer window to cast a shadow on the ceiling of the loft.

A pair of hand-carved oak griffins, left, came from a Victorian house in Chicago, where they connected the stoop railing to the porch railing. Here they have been attached to the front of a desk to make it the focus of this home office. It is obvious that they were hand carved because they are a bit different from each other.

When a Manhattan psychiatrist decided to open an office in his apartment, he realized that he needed to separate the kitchen from the area where he would see patients. Since he did not want to completely enclose the kitchen he searched for a solution that would screen the kitchen, but allow light and air to come in. He found these doors, above, which originally came from the headquarters of Lloyd's of London, the famous insurance company. Their frosted-glass insets allow light to come into the kitchen. The pine portions of the doors were stripped of paint and left in their natural color, which contrasts nicely with the oxidized bronze cames supporting and separating the glass panels.

    Another handsome door, left, that also once graced the offices of Lloyd's of London was used here on a pool house. The wooden portions were painted white to match the building, while the bronze cames, which separate the glass, catch the sunlight.

Columns can be reused to serve both a structural and an ornamental purpose. A large oak column, right, is one of two that support a loft balcony while at the same time creating a sense of separation between a dining area and a hallway. The color of the wood echoes that of the flooring, the furnishings, and the picture frames, creating a cohesive whole.

A pair of small columns, left, serves to carry the weight of the bookshelves in an elegant library. The vertical lines of the columns serve as counterpoint to the square and round forms of the adjacent artwork.

BRACKETS, BIG AND SMALL

Brackets come in all sizes, shapes, and materials. They were used as corbels to hold up cornices and balconies, to brace stair and porch railings, to frame posts, and to support roofs. Whether made of carved or sawed wood, cast or carved stone, cast or wrought iron, brackets are highly decorative and can be used in a multitude of ways, both as pure embellishment and as structural elements.

You can enliven a simple opening between two rooms by adding a pair of brackets, which are relatively simple to hang using storm-sash hangers or z-clips. The brackets can soften the hard geometric lines of an opening, or can help define a transition from one space to another.

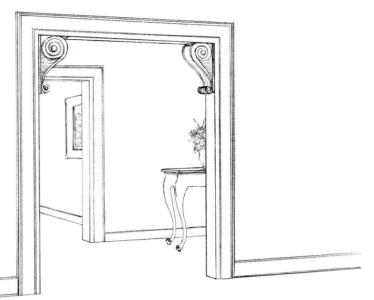

PASSAGEWAY

SHELF

Although brackets are usually found in sets, single ones often turn up. One bracket can easily serve as a support for a small table or shelf. The tabletop can be marble or, if you wish to see more of the bracket, plate glass.

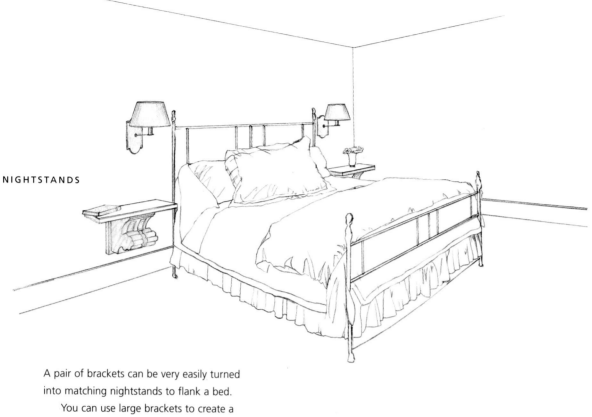

NIGHTSTANDS

A pair of brackets can be very easily turned
into matching nightstands to flank a bed.

You can use large brackets to create a
console table. Attach them directly to
the wall using storm sash hangers, and then
cover them with a piece of plate glass.

CONSOLE TABLE

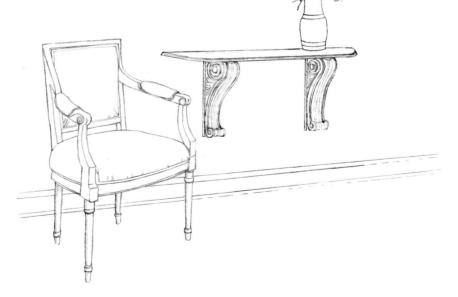

A pair of brackets can make a terrific support for a curtain rod. If your wooden brackets are large enough, you can drill a hole through them to support the rod. If you're using metal or stone brackets, you can attach a flange to the rod and then screw it into the side of the bracket. Paint rod, flange, and metal brackets all the same color so they will appear as a single unit, but leave stone brackets in their natural state.

CURTAIN ROD SUPPORT

ELEGANT OPTIONS FOR WOODEN FRAMES

Ornate wooden door and window frames are very commonly found in salvage. They can be quite simple or can have elaborate carving. Although they are generally tall and narrow, some wide frames that surrounded pocket doors or bay windows can also be found. Sometimes frames that have been removed from a single building will offer the same style in a variety of sizes, making it possible to create a number of pieces with a similar look.

Finding a wonderful new use for a fragment of a frame, particularly the architrave or top section, requires only a little imagination. Attaching returns to the sides will allow the piece to become an unusual and attractive curtain valance.

A door frame makes an elegant surround for a mirror. The mirror can be permanently affixed to the wall with the frame added on top, or the frame and mirror can be joined as a unit and then hung on a wall. If you can find a matching piece of frame or molding, you can add a bottom to the mirror, or if you want a shorter mirror, you can cut down the sides of the frame and use the pieces you removed to create a bottom for the mirror. In this way the wood will match. If you must fashion the bottom section from new wood, you will probably need to paint or refinish the entire piece.

MIRROR

BOOKCASE

Most frames are relatively flat, but you can make them more dimensional by adding a return. The depth of the return will depend upon the desired use. This bookcase features a frame providing an ornamental facing with a return of about 12 inches. The frame can be attached to the returns, which can in turn be affixed directly to a wall. Another possibility is to attach the returns to a backing and a base. This will create an independent piece of furniture that can be moved from one location to another.

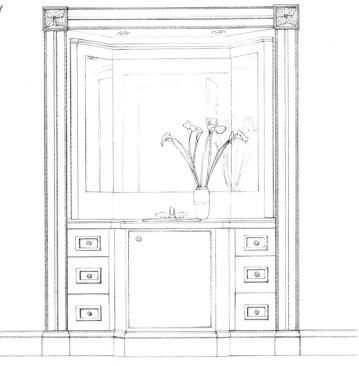

If frames can provide a decorative way to surround a door, they can just as well enclose other openings. A vanity set into a recess can be accented by a lovely wood frame fastened directly to the wall around the space.

You can also incorporate a fragment of a frame into a light fixture. Adding returns on the sides to hide the bulbs will allow the light to project upward and downward. The piece can be used as a wall sconce over a desk or a kitchen counter or over a bed as a reading light.

LIGHT FIXTURE

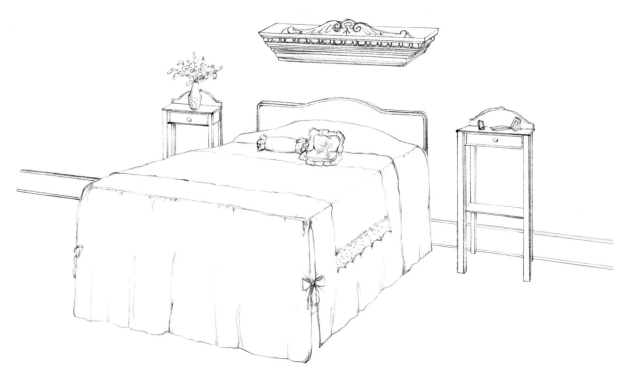

GLASS &

COMPOSITION

WHETHER IT IS STAINED, PAINTED, BEVELED, OR ETCHED, GLASS IS THE MOST POETIC

of materials used in architecture, altering with each passing cloud to define space

through light. The term "stained glass" denotes all decorative glass panels that have

color. This color can come from chemicals suspended in the molten glass to produce

relatively uniform color, from stains applied to finished glass and then fired, or from

colored enamel paint. Most stained-glass panels are mosaics of individual pieces of

glass held in place by metal rods that are soldered together. Called "cames," these

rods are traditionally made of lead, but occasionally copper, brass, or zinc is used.

The term "leaded glass" usually refers to decorative glass that has no color but

whose visual interest comes from the patterns and designs created by the metal

Previous page: Interior of the New York office of the Hamburg-American Line, 1908.

A leaded-glass window as beautiful as the one shown here is a rare find. All of the pieces of glass have beveled edges; the center and corner pieces have sunburst patterns that were wheel-cut and polished. To add to this decoration a series of heavily faceted "jewels" encircles the center. This window once sat above an entrance door; the side you are seeing was facing the outdoors. Now it hangs from the ceiling above the fireplace among a stunning collection of tribal artifacts.

holding the individual pieces of glass in place and by the beveling or engraving on the glass itself.

Glass has been produced for more than four thousand years. In architecture, its use dates from about the first century A.D., when glazing was first used in the homes of wealthy people living in northern Europe. At about the same time, glassmakers began experimenting with ways to alter the color and translucency of glass. The processes they developed, however, were hardly foolproof or exact; variations occurred from one batch of glass to another, which is what gives much old glass its character and interest.

As a building material, colored glass was originally reserved for churches. The development of colored and stained glass as a visual expression of Christian belief took place gradually, but by the eleventh and twelfth centuries there were many superb examples, including Augsburg Cathedral in Germany, the cathedral at Chartres in France, and Canterbury Cathedral in England. In fact, one of the earliest recorded examples of ornamental architectural salvage was of religious stained glass. When the original Romanesque church at Chartres was destroyed by fire in 1194, parishioners took the stained glass depicting the Virgin Mary, Nôtre Dame de la Belle Verrière, which had miraculously survived the fire, and reinstalled it as the centerpiece of a larger window in the rebuilt Gothic church, where it remains to this day.

It was in the Gothic churches that stained glass achieved its greatest glory. Soaring windows with pointed arches and enormous round windows were filled with colored and stained glass portraying the lives of the saints or telling biblical stories in intense colors and intricate patterns, allowing light to filter into the church interiors, inspiring the faithful and seducing the unbelievers. In the thirteenth century glassmakers discovered that applying a solution of silver nitrate to glass and then firing it at a high temperature would produce a golden color that permanently fused with the surface of the glass. This kind of glass is responsible for the exquisite glow that radiates from the saints in church windows.

Glassmaking in the United States was neither a successful business nor a flourishing art until almost the mid-nineteenth century; what little was used before then was imported from Europe. Early American churches tended to be simple and unadorned, with clear glass windows, a heritage of the Puritan beginnings of this country. But by the second half of the nineteenth century, the public's embrace of decoration coupled with improvements in glassmaking led to a tremendous surge in the production of high-quality domestic stained glass.

American artisans were, in fact, responsible for creating a whole new design vocabulary in glass, using it in highly inventive ways unknown to European glassmakers. No longer limited to churches, stained glass adorned even modest homes, usually as a transom over the entry door or in conjunction with sidelights flanking the door; many commercial buildings also had glass transoms over their entrances that gracefully incorporated the store name or street number into their design. Other common residential uses included decorative glass windows at staircase landings, fixed panes above operable windows, stained-glass panes in

These four stained-glass panels have been made into a room divider between the entry door and the living room in a contemporary home. They are held in place by redwood supports that echo the geometry of the living room windows. Attributed to George Grant Elmslie, an architect who was a disciple of Louis Sullivan and a contemporary of Frank Lloyd Wright, they are typical of stained glass from the Prairie school of architecture. The simple geometric shapes are supported by zinc cames rather than the traditional lead cames.

bathrooms where the occupants desired light but wished to obscure the view, decorative windows set into door panels, glass doors on china closets and cupboards, and door transoms between rooms. Mail-order catalogs from window manufacturers offered mass-produced designs for all these various uses at affordable prices.

The American Art Nouveau artists Louis Comfort Tiffany and John La Farge developed new glass-making techniques and improved traditional ones. Independently of one another, they pioneered the manufacture and use of opalescent glass, with milky streaks of variegated colors caused by internally refracted light. At the same time these

artists expanded the design possibilities of stained glass, producing windows that depicted complex naturalistic scenes; none of their works featured painted details but were rather painstakingly created using different-colored glass. Stained glass for churches and universities of the same era was usually produced in a neo-Gothic style, of which Charles J. Connick was the leader. Later, Frank Lloyd Wright and other architects of the Prairie style created stunning geometric designs in glass using zinc or bronze cames, which were much stiffer, stronger, and lighter than the traditional lead cames, allowing the designers to fabricate windows with fewer support bars.

A magnificent collection of
nineteenth-century glass objects
complements this unique stained
and heavily jeweled glass panel,
which once adorned the stairway
landing in a New York City
mansion built in the 1870s. The
current owner, a serious collector
of Moser glass, had searched
extensively for a window with the
ornate floral pattern, rich colors,
and exquisite jeweling that would
reflect the spirit of his glassware.
The window was installed in an
existing window frame where
it obscures an unwanted view yet
allows gently filtered and refracted
light to enter the dining room.

World War I saw a decline in the design of ornamental windows, largely because the lead and other metals needed for cames and framing were in scarce supply. After the war, stained glass once again became a material used primarily for religious or institutional purposes, and some of the finest artists of the era were commissioned to create stained-glass windows. Matisse, who created the Chapelle du Rosaire des Dominicaines de Vence in the South of France, and Marc Chagall, who designed the Lincoln Center in New York, are but two of the best-known examples.

The basic ingredient in glass is silica sand. To reduce the temperature required to melt the sand, an alkali is added, traditionally potash and more recently soda lime. The mixture is reduced to a liquid state and then shaped by blowing, pressing, drawing, floating, casting, or rolling; each method produces its own unique qualities. Most stained glass is made into sheets from a blown bubble of molten glass, which hardens as it cools. What is usually referred to as "stained glass" is actually colored glass—that is, glass that has had metal oxides added to silica in its molten state to produce a desired color; these additional substances alter the wavelengths of light passing through the glass, in turn altering the color of the glass.

Painted glass is just that, either clear or colored glass to which paint or stain has been applied. In decorative images, colored enamel paints could be applied to create the folds in garments, to add features to faces, or to suggest other details that could not be captured in glass alone. Stains were also used to add or modify color. Usually made from vitreous oxides in shades of black and brown, they were brushed on the hardened glass and then fired in a kiln to fuse them to the glass surface. Textures could be achieved as well, with etching, engraving, chipping, crackling, or crazing on the surface.

Finding a way to reuse a fragment of a stained-glass panel requires a bit of creativity. Above, an opening was cut in a simple wood door to fit around a fragment. The grapes in the glass give a hint of what is behind the door—a wine cellar.

Nedick's was a chain of fast-food restaurants that got its start in New York City in the 1920s and closed its last shop in the 1980s, a victim of the national fast-food chains. This ceramic sign, right, sat vertically under the service window of a Nedick's stand in the old Washington Market in lower Manhattan. The stand apparently started as a temporary structure but quickly became permanent: when the sign was removed, the entire stand collapsed. Here we see the sign inlaid like an old Roman mosaic in the marble counter of a contemporary kitchen.

In beveled glass the edges of plate glass are cut at some angle other than the usual ninety degrees. Bevels are created by grinding away excess glass at the desired angle; the ground edge is then polished in a series of progressively finer steps to achieve a smooth finish. Patterns can be incised into plate glass using stone or copper wheels, and then polished, if desired, to create a focal point or to accentuate the corners of the panels. Beveling and engraving add dimension to a glass design as well as allow the glass to refract light differently from smooth glass. Special panes of glass that have been faceted are said to have been "jeweled," and these very dimensional pieces are often found as highlights in the more elaborate designs from the American Victorian and Beaux Arts periods.

A wonderfully creative reuse of two broken stained-glass panels is shown here in a coffee table in a lovely country house. The two panels, which were each missing sections of glass and leading, were integrated to create one complete design. In the detail photographs the difference between the new leading and the original leading is easily visible; the designer, Elaine Bedell, wanted to acknowledge both the new and the old elements. The panel was then set into a custom-made wrought-iron frame and covered with a single piece of clear glass. The rich gold and blue hues of the glass echo beautifully the colors in the furnishings.

COMPOSITION AND PLASTER ORNAMENT

At one time or another we have all admired composition or plaster ornament without even knowing it, since those materials very frequently mimic carved wood as well as stone. The use of composition and plaster allowed repetitive decorative elements to be produced at a much lower cost than if they had been carved in wood or stone; it also permitted a degree of detail and intricacy rarely achieved in other materials. Related materials, such as papier-mâché and wood fiber, while not nearly as common as composition and plaster, were similarly used to create interior architectural details. Correctly identifying such materials is critical to the cleaning and restoration of objects made of them, since products and processes that work well with one material can do irreparable damage to another.

Composition ornament, often called "compo," is typically made from chalk, resins, glue, and linseed oil. When the ingredients are mixed together, they are soft and pliable; when fully dry, they are hard and rigid. Folding and kneading the mixture creates a dough of sorts, which is warmed in a steamer and then placed in a rigid mold that has been coated with oil and dusted with talcum powder. A damp board is placed over the dough, and pressure is applied to force the material down into the finest details in the mold. After the mold is removed, the compo is left to cool to a rubbery state and then cut off the board and either fixed to a prepared wooden substrate, or shipped to a site where it is steamed back into flexibility and installed on-site.

Similar processes have been used since the Renaissance to decorate wooden boxes and frames, but not until the end of the eighteenth century did compo become widely used for architectural decoration. The rise of the neoclassical movement in design in the United States, coupled with the availability of raw materials and experienced craftsmen, led to a surge in the use of compo to produce interior ornament in residential, commercial, and institutional settings. Mantels, wainscot panels, moldings, chair rails, and other flat, usually wooden, surfaces were often enhanced with intricate compo ornament. During the years of unrestrained interior ornamentation in the last half of the nineteenth century, the range of compo applications blossomed to include everything from coffered ceilings to carousel horses.

In salvaged ornament, composition is very often found on wooden mantels, paneling, wainscoting, and door and window frames. (If these items are painted, an unscrupulous or unknowing dealer can pass them off as wooden carving.) Old manufacturing molds are also available and can be lovely, especially the wooden ones.

Like compo, ornamental plaster was popular in the United States from the mid-eighteenth century to the 1930s. This material required essentially the same components and techniques that had been used since ancient Egypt. As the demand for ornamental plaster grew, so did the number of craftspeople and shops producing it; by the 1880s many plaster ornaments were available through mail-order catalogs. Ceiling coffering, medallions, cornices, and column capitals in various styles would be cast in molds in a shop and then assembled and installed in a building. For large

When the elevators at Lord and Taylor, the department store on Fifth Avenue in New York City, were modernized, the ornate cabs were removed. Here the dome that formed the top of a cab has been reused as the focal point of an elegant formal dining room. Although it looks like cast bronze it is actually composition ornament that has been gold leafed, reflecting the light of the chandelier.

Salvaged ornament often gains interest from the changes that have been wrought in it over time. This mirror within a plaster shell came from an early French movie theater and has been converted into a wall sconce. The silvering on the mirror has aged, making it look almost like mother-of-pearl and allowing small rays of light to peek through. The lamps are fixed to the wall behind the sconce, and a hole was cut in the back of the plaster so that the fixture rests on the structure holding the bulbs.

architectural elements such as balcony fronts or columns, the plaster would be reinforced with a coarse weave cloth as it was built up in the molds.

The most sublime examples of plaster ornamentation come from the grand theaters of the 1920s and 1930s. The material was used so extensively in some theaters that a shop for casting was sometimes set up on-site. This extravagant use of plaster—often combined with compo and usually covered with paint, glazes, or gilding—created the delicious fantasylike quality of these theatrical palaces.

Plaster was also used to fabricate molds for plaster and terra-cotta ornament, and stone carvers would sometimes have plaster models produced of sculptures for approval by the owner or architect prior to starting work. These molds and models can occasionally be found in architectural salvage.

Other materials were used to create applied interior ornamentation, but they never became as popular as compo and plaster. Papier-mâché ornament, made from soaked paper combined with a starch binder and layered into molds, can sometimes be found in architectural salvage. Often covered with whiting and glue and then gilded, it can be distinguished from compo and plaster by the hollow sound it makes when gently tapped. Midway between papier-mâché and plaster is carton pierre, made from paper fiber extended and hardened with glue, whiting, and gypsum plaster or sometimes alum and flour to form a mixture that was pressed into molds and then allowed to harden. Finally, sawdust combined with various binders was sometimes used in the nineteenth century to produce small architectural decorations.

This cherub once looked down at elegant dining and dancing in the ballroom of New York City's Pierre Hotel, which opened in 1929. It was removed with about forty other cherubs during the first of several renovations. Made of papier-mâché and gilded with gold leaf, it weighs about 8 pounds. Picture wire secured to the brick wall is attached to a screw eye in its back, while the cherub's toe balances it off the wall. The other cherubs make an appearance every Christmas season at Macy's flagship store in New York City as part of the store's holiday decorations.

This staine[...]
originally [...]
of a French [...]
around the [...]
now rests [...]
the same e[...]
hinged for [...]
with simpl[...]
bars behin[...]
were paint[...]
fired rathe[...]
to the glas[...]
delicate re[...]
were added[...]

Two small glass panels, left, with delicate and intricate leading have been hinged together and then hinged to one side of an opening between a kitchen and a living room to create the door to a pass-through. When the door is closed, the leading provides interest and also partially obscures the view into the kitchen.

Composed of hundreds of individual pieces of colored glass, a stunning mosaic, opposite, picks up every shift in light as the sun moves through a garden. The mosaic panel has been set into a piece of marble, which in turn has been installed in a brick wall. Although the mosaic came from a church, the image is secular; it appears to be a celebration of the harvest, with a bunch of grapes and a sheaf of wheat. The colors are particularly vivid, with the rich purple of the grapes set against the gold of the background, symbolizing perhaps the power of the sun to make crops grow.

A CORPORATE HOME FOR ORNAMENT

Although companies have always purchased artworks and sponsored art projects, widespread corporate art programs really began in the 1970s when corporations moved into large modern buildings with miles and miles of white corridors. Having traded traditional interior ornamentation for minimalist designs, planners needed to find new ways to enhance their spaces. The cost of original paintings and sculpture was rising, and at the same time the definition of "art" was changing. Photography, folk art, and ethnic art thus became part of the mainstream, and corporations also began to collect architectural details.

Many companies now have architectural pieces in their collections, and some have used ornament extensively. Barbara Berger, a corporate art consultant who has used decorative architectural details in many of her projects, expresses a common sentiment when she says, "Architectural pieces work well in any environment. They are beautiful, have great presence and wonderful historic reference. They speak of another time and are a vanishing art form—they should be savored and not lost."

A magnificent copper lion keeps watch over the boardroom at the law firm of Herrick, Feinstein in New York. His color adds richness to an otherwise monochromatic room, and his shape fills the wall space beautifully. He formed a portion of the cornice of the Fireman's Fund Building in lower Manhattan until he was removed in 1983.

One of the entrances to the New York City headquarters of the investment bank Rothschild, Inc., is graced by a circular cast-iron grille, 61 inches in diameter, that originally came from the ceiling of the Union Square Theater in Manhattan. An extremely impressive installation has been achieved by placing the grille on a round panel to enhance its dimensionality and echo the circular shape of the lighting cove in the ceiling above. The grille has not been restored; the mottling of rust visible through the white paint creates a much more interesting effect than if it had been stripped and repainted.

At either end of the boardroom at Rothschild, Inc., is a cast-aluminum panel that was removed from the
Barbizon Hotel in New York City. The panel pictured here represents art; the one at the other end of the room
represents music. Both panels have been set into black anodized aluminum frames to reinforce their status
as works of art, a sentiment that is echoed throughout Rothschild's art program.

In corporate offices, just as in private homes, there are two approaches to displaying architectural ornament. The most common method is to hang details as art, as they would be in a museum. The scale of large architectural pieces is particularly appropriate for the long corridors and large reception spaces inherent in offices.

Another approach is to integrate the details into new construction. When Best Products built their new corporate headquarters in McLean, Virginia, they built into the facade an enormous eagle's head that had been salvaged from the demolished Airline Terminal Building in New York City. It is even easier to integrate details into interior construction, as was done by Wilcox Associates (see pages 106–7) and Citibank (see page 192).

The law library at Herrick, Feinstein is illuminated by a handsome Art Deco bronze-and-glass bank deposit stand and light. The light originally shone on customers who banked at the Brooklyn branch of the former Manufacturer's Trust Company.

Probably the most passionate corporate collector of architectural elements is Herrick, Feinstein, a law firm in New York City that owns close to fifty exceptional pieces. The elements are presented museum style, complete with descriptive plaques, historic photos of the elements in their original surroundings, and a catalog detailing selected items. Edward Abramson, one of the partners, says, "We thought that we had some obligation to the past to retain some vestiges of it."

Since Herrick, Feinstein represents many real estate developers, these pieces also pro-

Separated from the late-nineteenth-century New York residence where it originally sat, this pine gable louver, left, looks like a contemporary painting. Only when you get close to it do you see the weathered wood and faded paint that mark it as an architectural piece.

In keeping with their overall theme, Herrick, Feinstein has cleverly used an old doorknob, below, from a New York public school to identify the key to their rest rooms.

vide a link to their clients, who are hopefully building the next generation of landmarks. Reception areas, conference rooms, hallways, and even doorways to the rest rooms exhibit architectural elements. Mounted on a column near the entrance to the law library, for example, is a section of railing that was removed from the Brooklyn Bridge as part of the renovation program prior to the bridge's centennial celebration in 1983. States the law firm in its catalog, "Yes, even attorneys will succumb to an offer to buy a piece of the Brooklyn Bridge."

Sitting in the main reception area of Rothschild, Inc., like a modern abstract painting is a cast-aluminum panel, above left, that was a spandrel from the former Airline Terminal Building in Manhattan. An eagle from the same building was integrated into the headquarters of Best Products in Richmond, Virginia.

In each of the interior corner offices and conference areas at Herrick, Feinstein, niches were created to hold a keystone, above right. Each keystone is different, but all are typical of the terra-cotta ornament that once sat above the window and door arches in turn-of-the-century urban row houses.

Soaring in the stairwell of Herrick, Feinstein is a carved wooden eagle, left, that originally sat over the bench of the Federal Courthouse building in Philadelphia, which was demolished in the early 1980s. A metal bracket, painted white to match the wall, holds the eagle in place. Because the bracket is visible only from certain angles, and then only when you look carefully, the magnificient eagle actually appears to be flying, often surprising visitors to the office.

Samuel Yellin was probably the greatest and best-known ironworker in the United States. He arrived in America in 1906 at the age of twenty-one, having become a master craftsman in his native Poland. Although Yellin died in 1940, his shop in the Philadelphia area is still in operation. One of his creations, this set of wrought-iron gates from a town house on East Sixty-fourth Street in New York City, has been integrated into the entrance to the offices of a venture capital firm related to Citicorp. It is a wonderful example of Yellin's trademark method of joining individual iron elements with loose links, similar to chain mail, rather than with rigid welds.

RESOURCES

FINDING AND PURCHASING

Architectural ornament can be purchased from a number of sources. Where you shop will depend on your experience and knowledge, the quality and scarcity of the ornament you are seeking, and where you live. The following list provides brief descriptions of the kinds of outlets for these pieces, how to find them, and what to expect from each type.

DEALERS IN ARCHITECTURAL ORNAMENT

There are dealers just about everywhere now who specialize in architectural items. Some do the actual salvage work themselves; others just sell the ornament. Reputable dealers are a good source for the novice. They offer the widest selection of ornament, and the people working there will most likely know where their pieces come from. They usually can provide recommendations for repair, restoration, installation, and even shipping. Experienced, specialized outlets like Irreplaceable Artifacts and others around the country have a wealth of ideas and expertise in finding new uses for their pieces and can provide assistance in realizing your projects.

You can track down these dealers through restoration publications. Two good ones are *The Old House Journal* and *Traditional Building*, both of which deal with old buildings and historic methods of construction. They also contain ads for dealers, restoration experts, and places that make reproductions. Design publications such as *Interior Digest* and *Metropolis* carry ads for dealers too, as do some other trade publications.

ANTIQUES DEALERS

General antiques dealers sometimes have architectural pieces. Many carry lighting fixtures and mantels, and some are expanding into ornamental detail. These items are not their specialty, however, and so the staff will not necessarily be familiar with the materials or the potential applications of the pieces. For them, a mantel is something you use around the opening of a fireplace, not as a headboard, a pass-through, or a piece of furniture.

MUNICIPAL SALVAGE YARDS

A number of cities have started up their own salvage operations, reselling items saved from city-owned buildings that have been demolished. In most instances, purchases can be made only with proof of residency, such as a utility bill. The staff will usually know where the items come from and what they are made of, but will probably not have much experience in creatively reusing the pieces. Check with your local preservation organization to find out if there is a municipal salvage yard in your area.

OTHER SOURCES

Architectural antiques are starting to show up at antiques shows, flea markets, and auctions on a fairly regular basis. Check your local newspapers as well as design and trade magazines for dates and locations. Occasionally yard sales will yield architectural items, but you are unlikely to get substantive information about the pieces.

SHOPPING TIPS

You should always bring along a few items when you go shopping for ornament. Although some dealers may have one or all of these, don't count on it—bring your own. Depending on the object you are looking for, you may not need all of these tools, but here are some suggestions:

A tape measure, preferably an 8-foot steel tape like the ones used by carpenters, is indispensable. In conjunction with graph paper, the tape will allow you to record the size and overall shape of a particular piece, in case you need to verify whether it will fit in your intended space.

When you're looking for metal items, a magnet will help you determine if a material has iron in it, which may be difficult to tell if the piece is painted or has been galvanized. If the magnet sticks to a piece of metal, then it has iron, whether cast or wrought iron, steel or stainless steel. A magnet will not stick to brass, bronze, tin, zinc, copper, lead, nickel, or aluminum.

If you are looking for a piece to fit in a particular spot, you should measure that area and bring the dimensions with you when you shop. If you have a photograph or architectural drawings, even better.

Remember, ornamental details are often one-of-a-kind items, so be prepared to make a decision on the spot; if you hesitate, the piece may be sold to someone else before you return.

Be prepared to be flexible; don't expect to find the exact piece you have in mind, since each piece is slightly different. With enough creativity, many different kinds of ornament in a variety of materials can be adapted to fit a space and can surpass in beauty any ideas you might have had when you started.

Don't be discouraged by the weight of some of these objects, especially those made of stone. When set into masonry, they may need no additional support. When hung on sheetrock walls, they may actually require no more structural support than a set of bookshelves.

RESTORING AND REPAIRING

When looking at any architectural detail, decide whether or not you can live with it as is. The former life of any given detail is part of its attraction, so rust, flaking paint, and dings and dents can add personality and character. A restored piece actually may not look as good as a weathered piece, especially if it's made of a material that develops a patina such as copper or brass. Layers of paint soften edges and corners, so be aware that if you strip off the paint, the character of the piece may change. Other pieces may not have aged well at all and may have lost a level of detail over time. This is especially true of sandstone ornament that was improperly carved.

One word of caution regarding painted ornament: It is a good idea to have the paint tested for lead, especially if there is any chance that a small child will come in contact with it. If it tests positive, you must decide whether to leave the paint as it is—but do so *only* if it is not flaking—or to strip it or seal it.

Although facade elements were meant to be used outdoors, some care in their installation is still necessary. On the original building these pieces were installed upright and were usually protected by an overhang or cornice. When you install stone pieces outside, make sure that no water will collect in the depressions. Standing water, especially in the winter when it freezes, can wreak havoc on stone and terra cotta.

Restoration and repair of architectural details is an art in itself. The following tips may be helpful, but for any major project, you should consult a specialist in that particular material or process. In general, the best rule of thumb for cleaning any piece is to start with the gentlest technique, preferably in a small area that is not visible, and then try progressively more aggressive methods, testing each new procedure in a small area before attempting to clean the entire piece.

METAL OBJECTS

First of all you must determine what the actual metal is. Then decide what degree of restoration is desirable or necessary. If you strip off the paint, will the piece be repainted, sealed with a clear lacquer to prevent future weathering, or left in its natural state? The final finish will also depend on whether the piece will be used indoors or outside.

Techniques for cleaning, stripping, polishing, plating, and finishing are different for each of the metals. In addition, many of the chemicals and techniques used are highly toxic and need to be used under controlled conditions. It is therefore recommended that you consult a professional in the field for best results.

While it is not unusual to find metal pieces that have received proper care over the years and are therefore in excellent condition, many items will need repair. The bottoms of doors, fences, and gates, for instance, are a common area for decay, so these portions may need to be replaced or rebuilt. The expense is generally not significant, and there are many experienced craftspeople who can do the work (see Sources for Restoration). Metal pieces can be cut, added to, or set into a frame to make them fit within a desired space, so don't be discouraged if you can't find a ready-made piece with the exact dimensions you need.

More information is available in the most authoritative and useful book on the subject, *Metals in America's Historic Buildings: Part 1, A Historical Survey of Metals; Part II, Deterioration and Methods of Preservating Metal*, by Margot Gayle, David W. Look, and John Wait, published by Preservation Assistance Division, National Parks Service, U.S. Department of Interior.

DECORATIVE GLASS

In general, almost any piece of decorative glass can be easily repaired or restored by a qualified professional. Other than cleaning, no glass restoration can be done by a layperson. When looking at stained glass it is important to check for a milky film that seems to disappear when the glass is wet but returns when it dries. Referred to as "chalking," this problem is caused by exposure to sunlight and various atmospheric elements. Decide if you can live with it, because this film cannot be removed.

Check also to see if the cames—the metal frames around the pieces of glass—are cracked and if the solder holding the cames together is still solid. Zinc, brass, and copper cames, which were popular for Prairie-style windows because they are stiffer than the traditional lead cames, are beveled rather than butted at their joints. This means that in order to replace a single piece of glass in one of these windows, the worker must disassemble the entire window. Also, when you're looking at beveled windows with cracked glass, be aware that any replacements will be very difficult and expensive to replicate exactly. Decide if the crack is something that you can live with; if not, try to get a cost estimate for the repair before you purchase the piece.

An excellent resource guide is *Great Glass in American Architecture: Decorative Windows and Doors Before 1920* by Weber H. Wilson, published in 1983 by Dutton.

STONE

Generally it is best to accept a stone ornament in the condition in which you find it. You might make an exception if there is so much paint that details are obscured or if graffiti or carbon deposits mar the appearance of the object. Carbon can accentuate details if it heightens the contrast on light-colored stone such as limestone or white terra cotta, but some people prefer to remove it. Professionals who do paint stripping are usually not equipped to work on stone, but the recent rise in the number of experts in historic preservation has created a pool of people with expertise in this area (see Sources for Restoration).

The best and simplest method of cleaning most stone is soap and water applied with a small scrub brush. Stone pieces that are broken can sometimes be joined with epoxy, but missing ears, noses, and other carved parts are costly to replicate. Before transporting a stone detail, wrap it carefully in blankets to protect it; carved details that project from the face are quite susceptible to damage.

Many stone pieces will have some of the mortar that held it in place still attached. You can use a flat bar or a wide mason's chisel to scrape or lightly tap off this excess. Terra-cotta details may have bricks in the honeycomb spaces in back; you can remove these the same way, always exercising great care and being as gentle as possible.

WOOD ORNAMENT

Unless they are completely rotted or termite infested, architectural elements made from wood can generally be restored easily. Even broken carvings can be replicated and replaced. Staining, bleaching, pickling, burnishing, distressing, and ebonizing can alter the final surface appearance to suit any taste or match any environment.

It is important to verify if what appears to be carving on wood, especially on mantels and moldings, is actually made of wood or if it is made of molded composition. The accurate identification of composition ornament is critical to the cleaning and restoration of wood details. Products and processes that work well on wood may irreparably damage the decorative detail in composition materials, which are best cleaned by a professional.

SOURCES FOR RESTORATION

PUBLICATIONS

OLD HOUSE JOURNAL

Dovetail Publishers
The Blackburn Tavern
2 Main Street
Gloucester, MA 01930
Subscriptions: 800-234-3797
Information: 508-281-8803

This publication is useful on two levels. It has technical articles on historical materials and building methods that can have application to architectural details. It also carries advertisements for products and services such as period and reproduction hardware, tin ceilings, antique flooring, dealers in architectural ornament, and reproductions. The magazine, published six times a year, produces *The OHJ Restoration Directory*, listing over 1,500 products and services for renovation.

THIS OLD HOUSE

20 West 43rd Street
New York, NY 10036
Subscriptions: 800-898-7237
Information: 212-522-9465

The companion magazine to the popular television program, this bimonthly publication often carries helpful articles on materials, processes, and other issues related to historic buildings. It also contains ads for relevant products and services.

TRADITIONAL BUILDING

Historical Trends Corporation
69A Seventh Avenue
Brooklyn, NY 11217
Information and subscriptions:
718-636-0788

This oversize publication, issued six times a year, bills itself as "the professional's source for historical products." Editor and publisher Clem Labine was the original publisher of the *Old House Journal*, the great-granddaddy of magazines about living with historic properties. Each issue highlights a particular topic and contains several short technical articles; a list of suppliers, fabricators, or artisans in a particular specialty; and advertisements for products and services relevant to the restoration of historic properties. Many of these same products and professionals can be helpful in the restoration of architectural details.

THE BUILDING CONSERVATION DIRECTORY

Cathedral Communications Limited
The Old Brewery, Tisbury
Wiltshire SP3 6NH
England
E-mail @ cathcomm.demon.co.uk

A directory of consultants, craftspeople, suppliers, and organizations involved in building preservation in England.

PERIOD LIVING & TRADITIONAL HOMES

Tower Publishing Services
Tower House
Sovereign Park, Market Harborough
Leicester LE16 9EF
Telephone: 01858 468888

A monthly publication that includes information on restoration of traditional buildings and materials.

SALVOMAGAZINE

Produced every month or two, this magazine by the same publishers as *SalvoNEWS* covers topics of interest to architects, landscapers, and homeowners about architectural and garden antiques, reclaimed building materials, conservation, and green building. Both of these publications can be ordered from:

Ford Woodhouse
Berwick Upon Tweed TD15 2QF
England
Telephone: 00 44 1668 216494
They can also be reached on their web page, SolvoWEB, at
http://www.salvo.co.uk.

SALVONEWS

A biweekly newsletter geared to dealers in architectural and garden antiques as well as reclaimed building materials.

PRESERVATION ORGANIZATIONS

Local and state preservation organizations often certify contractors to work on historic buildings. They may also maintain list of qualified professionals. The New York Landmarks Conservancy, for example, publishes a guide called *Restoration Directory: A Listing of Services in the New York City Area*, which it updates every few years with the names and addresses of building consultants, specialists in the restoration of materials, and even a list of architectural salvage companies. You can find your local preservation organization in the telephone book or in the *Landmark Yellow Pages*, a publication of the National Trust for Historic Preservation, published by John Wiley and Sons.

CATALOG SALES

There has been a boom in suppliers of materials for restoration and renovation in the past several years. They all advertise in the magazines listed above. Two companies in particular have been around for a while and are quite reputable.

DECORATORS SUPPLY CORP.

3610-12 South Morgan Street
Chicago, IL 60609
Telephone: 312-847-6300
Fax: 312-847-6357

In business since the turn of the century, this company offers 14,000 patterns for period architectural elements and molded ornament in plaster, composition, and wood.

RENOVATORS SUPPLY

Box 2515
Conway, NH 03818-2515
Telephone: 800-659-0203

This is a good source for reproduction period hardware.

An excellent reference to find mail-order sources and artisans producing ornament is Brent Brolin's *Sourcebook of Architectural Ornament: Designers, Craftsmen, Manufacturers and Distributors of Custom and Readymade Exterior Ornament*, published in 1982 by Van Nostrand.

ASSOCIATIONS

The Preservation Assistance Division of the National Park Service has a wealth of technical information about historic materials. Their publication, *The Catalog of Historic Preservation Publications: Guidance on the Treatment of Historic Properties*, lists over 100 books, as well as Preservation Briefs, Preservation Tech Notes, videotapes, and other materials concerning historic properties and materials. For a free copy, write NPS-PAD, PubCat, P.O. Box 37127, Washington, DC 20013-7127

The following NPS publications are of particular interest and can be ordered, for a nominal fee, from the Government Printing Office:

PRESERVATION BRIEF 7:
The Preservation of Historic Glazed Architectural Terra Cotta

PRESERVATION BRIEF 23:
Preserving Historic Ornamental Plaster

PRESERVATION BRIEF 27:
The Maintenance and Repair of Architectural Cast Iron

PRESERVATION BRIEF 33:
The Preservation and Repair of Historic Stained and Leaded Glass

PRESERVATION BRIEF 34:
Applied Decoration for Historic Interiors

FRIENDS OF CAST-IRON ARCHITECTURE

235 East 87th Street, 6C
New York, NY 10128
212-369-6004

This national organization was established in 1970 to gather public support to preserve surviving examples of cast-iron architecture.

FRIENDS OF TERRA COTTA

c/o Tunick
771 West End Avenue, Suite 10E
New York, NY 10025
212-932-1750

This national nonprofit organization was founded to promote education and research in the preservation of architectural terra cotta and related ceramic materials. The organization seeks to educate construction-industry professionals and the general public about architectural terra cotta's history and value as a building material. They offer a number of publications and sponsor walking tours in New York City, highlighting buildings incorporating terra cotta.

NATIONAL ORNAMENTAL & MISC. METALS ASSOCIATION

804-10 Main Street
Suite E
Forest Park, GA 30050
404-363-4009
(fax: 404-366-1852)

This trade association of 650 metal fabricators will provide a list of its members in your area if you are seeking a qualified fabricator.

NATIONAL TRUST FOR HISTORIC PRESERVATION

1785 Massachusetts Avenue, NW
Washington, DC 20036
202-673-4000

The National Trust is a private organization chartered by Congress to encourage public participation in the preservation of sites, buildings, and objects significant in American history. A subscription to the magazine *Historic Preservation* is a benefit of membership.

ENGLISH HERITAGE

Fortress House
23 Savile Row
London W1X 1RB
Phone: 0171 387 1721

INSTITUTE OF ADVANCED ARCHITECTURAL STUDIES

University of York
King's Manor
York YO1 2EP, England
01904 433 963

The institute offers weeklong courses on using and restoring traditional building materials.

USED BUILDING MATERIALS ASSOCIATION

2-70 Albert Street
Winnipeg, Manitoba R3B1ET
204-947-0848

This is a newly formed organization of businesses involved in salvaging architectural material, from ornamental details to mechanical equipment.

MUSEUMS

Most museums in the United States and Europe have some architectural ornament in their collections, either as period rooms or as part of their sculpture collections. In general these examples are either extremely old or from famous buildings. The Metropolitan Museum of Art in New York has numerous pieces in their American Wing, and the Victoria and Albert Museum in London has departments that feature ironwork, stained glass, and tiles. The following museums, however, are of particular interest because of the nature or breadth of their collections of architectural details.

THE ANONYMOUS ARTS MUSEUM

Charlotteville, NY 12036
607-397-8276

This is the only museum in the world devoted entirely to the display of decorative architectural elements. Most of its pieces are stone carvings rescued from demolished buildings. It is open each year from mid-June to the end of August, only on weekends.

BROOKLYN MUSEUM

200 Eastern Parkway
Brooklyn, NY 11238-6052
718-638-5000

This was the first museum to actively exhibit exterior architectural details from demolished buildings. The Frieda Schiff Warburg Memorial Sculpture Garden, established in 1966, houses over three hundred pieces in a tranquil, leafy environment.

CHICAGO ART INSTITUTE

111 South Michigan Avenue
Chicago, IL 60603-6110
312-443-3600

The trading room and the entrance arch from the demolished Chicago Stock Exchange by Adler and Sullivan have been reconstructed at the Art Institute. A collection of architectural details called "Fragments of Old Chicago" is also on permanent display.

MUSEUM OF THE UNIVERSITY OF SOUTHERN ILLINOIS AT EDWARDSVILLE

SIEU Campus Box 1150
Edwardsville, IL 62026
618-692-2996

The university's museum houses several hundred pieces of ornament, mostly from buildings designed by Louis Sullivan. Many of the items were salvaged by the architectural photographer Richard Nickel.

NATIONAL ORNAMENTAL METAL MUSEUM

374 Metal Museum Drive
Memphis, TN 38106-1539
901-774-6380

The only museum in the United States dedicated exclusively to the exhibition and preservation of fine metalwork, this institution has a sculpture garden featuring work by metal artists from around the world. A highlight is the Riverbluff Pavilion, constructed with castings rescued from a building that stood on historic Beale Street in the 1800s. In addition to the permanent collection, there are special temporary exhibitions, metalworking demonstrations, and classes for local residents. The museum offers conservation and restoration services to other institutions.

WOLFSONIAN FOUNDATION

1001 Washington Avenue
Miami Beach, FL 33139
305-531-1001

Opened in 1995, the Wolfsonian over-sees the Mitchell Wolfson Jr. Collection of nineteenth- and twentieth-century art and design. Housed in a renovated 1927 Art Deco landmark warehouse, it displays over twenty different kinds of rescued architectural elements, along with art-work from its collection

AVON CROFT
MUSEUM OF BUILDING

Stoke Prior
Near Bromsgrove
Worcestershire B60 4JR, England
01527 831 386

This open-air building museum includes the National Telephone Kiosk Collection, with all those lovely red boxes.

BUILDING OF BATH

Countess of Huntingdon's Chapel
The Vineyards, The Paragon
Bath BA1 5NA, England
01225 333 895

A permanent exhibition explains how the city of Bath was constructed at a time when architecture was not yet a profession and craftsmen had far greater influence on the way buildings were built. Along with scale models of a typical Georgian house there are salvaged pieces of joinery, plaster, wallpaper, carvings, and other practi-cal or ornamental details.

THE CHARLES BROOKING COLLECTION

Greenwich University
Oakfield Lane
Dartford DA1 2S, England
0181 33 9897

Thirty years ago, Charles Brooking started collecting architectural details that he rescued from demolished buildings. The collection has grown to be the most significant in the United Kingdom, with over 7000 items that come from all building types, from the grandest mansions to rural cottages, as well as industrial and commercial buildings. The collection includes examples of doors, windows, fire-places, staircase sections, balustrades, architraves, skirtings, sash boxes, and glazing bars that come from England, Wales, Scotland, and Ireland. There is both a permanent display of a cross section of the collection and a reserve study section. The exhibition can be viewed by appointment with the keeper, Julie Wakefield.

MUSÉE LE SECQ
DES TOURNELLES

2, rue Jacques Villon
76008 Rouen, France
2-35-88-42-92

Housed in the Church of Saint-Laurent, built in the sixteenth century in what is today the historic center of Rouen, this museum houses 15,000 pieces of ornamental ironwork dating from the seventeenth to the nine-teenth century and constituting the largest collection in the world.

SIR JOHN SOANE MUSEUM

12 Lincoln's Inns Fields
London EC1, England
0171 405 2107

This is the collection of Sir John Soane, an architect who amassed several thou-sand items, mostly architectural, dating from the Egyptian era through the early 1800s. They are exhibited as Soane had done, in his own home, which is now the museum.

BIBLIOGRAPHY

The following is a sampling of books that document the destruction of our architectural legacy:

Brumfield, William Craft, LOST RUSSIA: PHOTOGRAPHING THE RUINS OF RUSSIAN ARCHITECTURE. Durham: Duke University Press, 1995.

Cable, Mary, LOST NEW ORLEANS. New York: American Legacy Press, 1984.

Cahan, Richard, THEY ALL FALL DOWN: RICHARD NICKEL'S STRUGGLE TO SAVE AMERICA'S ARCHITECTURE. Washington, D.C.: The Preservation Press, 1994.

Dendy, William, LOST TORONTO. Toronto: Oxford University Press, 1978.

Eveno, Claude, PARIS PERDU. Paris: Editions Carré, 1995.

Greiff, Constance M., LOST AMERICA: FROM THE ATLANTIC TO THE MISSISSIPPI. Princeton, N.J.: The Pyne Press, 1971.

————, LOST AMERICA: FROM THE MISSISSIPPI TO THE PACIFIC. Princeton, N.J.: The Pyne Press, 1972.

Hobhouse, Hermione, LOST LONDON: A CENTURY OF DEMOLITION AND DECAY. London: Macmillan, 1972.

Iberville-Moreau, Luc d', LOST MONTREAL. Toronto: Oxford University Press, 1975.

Jones, Carlton, LOST BALTIMORE LANDMARKS: A PORTFOLIO OF VANISHED BUILDINGS. Baltimore: Maclay, 1982.

Kaplan, Sam Hall, L.A., LOST AND FOUND: AN ARCHITECTURAL HISTORY OF LOS ANGELES. New York: Crown, 1987.

Kay, Jane Holtz, LOST BOSTON. Boston: Houghton Mifflin, 1980.

Keegan, Susanne, LOST BERLIN. New York: St. Martin's Press. 1979.

Lowe, David, LOST CHICAGO. New York: American Legacy Press, 1985.

Millet, Larry, LOST TWIN CITIES. St. Paul: Minnesota Historical Society Press, 1992.

Silver, Nathan, LOST NEW YORK. Boston: Houghton Mifflin, 1967.

Strong, Roy C., THE DESTRUCTION OF THE COUNTRY HOUSE. London: Thames and Hudson, 1974.

For additional information about architectural ornament, both in general and in specific cities:

Adamson, Anthony, THE GAIETY OF GABLES: ONTARIO'S ARCHITECTURAL FOLK ART. Toronto: McClelland & Stewart, 1974.

Architectural Conservancy of Ontario, TERRA COTTA: ARTFUL DECEIVERS. Toronto: Architectural Conservancy of Ontario, 1990.

Barnard, Julian, THE DECORATIVE TRADITION. London: Architectural Press, 1973.

Bayer, Patricia, ART DECO ARCHITECTURE: DESIGN, DECORATIONS AND DETAIL FROM THE TWENTIES AND THIRTIES. New York: Harry Abrams, 1992.

Brolin, Brent, FLIGHT OF FANCY: THE BANISHMENT AND RETURN OF ORNAMENT. New York: St. Martin's, 1985.

Ferriday, Virginia Guest, LAST OF THE HANDMADE BUILDINGS: GLAZED TERRA COTTA IN DOWNTOWN PORTLAND. Portland, Ore.: Mark Publishing Company, 1984.

Haldane, Suzanne, FACES ON PLACES. New York: Viking Press, 1980.

Jacoby, Stephen M., ARCHITECTURAL SCULPTURE IN NEW YORK CITY. New York: Dover Publications, Inc., 1975.

Karp, Ben, ORNAMENTAL CARPENTRY ON NINETEENTH-CENTURY AMERICAN HOUSES. New York: Dover Publications, 1981.

King, Stephen, and f-stop Fitzgerald, NIGHTMARES IN THE SKY: GARGOYLES AND GROTESQUES. New York: Viking Penguin Inc., 1988.

Kobayashi, Yukimo, and Ryo Watanabe, NEW YORK DETAIL; A TREASURY OF ORNAMENTAL SPLENDOR. New York: Chronicle Books, 1995.

Rooney, William A, ARCHITECTURAL ORNAMENTATION IN CHICAGO. Chicago: Chicago Review Press, 1984.

Rosen, Laura, TOP OF THE CITY: NEW YORK'S HIDDEN ROOFTOP WORLD. New York: Thames and Hudson, 1990.

Weinreb, Matthew, LONDON ARCHITECTURE: FEATURES AND FAÇADES. London: Phaidon Press Ltd., 1993.

Woodbridge, Sally Byrne, DETAILS: THE ARCHITECT'S ART. San Francisco: Chronicle Books, 1991.

Yang, John, OVER THE DOOR: THE ORNAMENTAL STONEWORK OF NEW YORK. New York: Princeton Architectural Press, 1995.

ACKNOWLEDGMENTS

Everyone who helped make this book possible has one thing in common—a love for architectural ornament. They care about saving historic buildings, rescuing ornaments when buildings must be demolished or altered, and most important, finding new uses for these decorative elements so that they will continue to be part of our lives.

Our first and greatest thanks goes to all of the wonderful people who allowed us to photograph their homes and offices. Without their imagination and cooperation, this book would not be possible.

The idea for this book originated with our editor at Clarkson Potter, Annetta Hanna. She approached us about doing this project and then supplied the technical and moral support necessary to make it a reality. Many others at Clarkson Potter helped make this book the best that it could be, including Amy Boorstein, Robbin Gourley, Howard Klein, Jane Searle, Lauren Shakely, and Jane Treuhaft. Our thanks also go to the designer of this book, Constance Old and our illustrator, Lydia Romero.

Jennifer Greenberg, stylist extraordinaire, taught us some of the tricks of the trade and shared her sources with us. Among those sources was Maxine Kaplan at the Prop Company, who kindly lent us many delightful items for our photographs.

Barbara Head Millstein at the Brooklyn Museum gave generously of her time and her wealth of knowledge, which forms the basis of the section in this book about stone carving. Ivan and Marilynn Karp warmly welcomed us into their museum and into their home, and shared their memories and anecdotes about rescuing ornament over the last forty years.

Within the preservation community, many individuals and organizations provided technical information and contacts: Judith Saltzman of Li-Saltzman Architects lent us helpful books about historic building materials and offered much useful advice along with a dose of her usual good humor; Roger P. Lang of the New York Landmarks Conservancy gave us technical manuals produced by the Conservancy; Susan Tunick of the Friends of Terra Cotta also told us about helpful books.

Gordon Henderson, whose father and grandfather before him were in the stained-glass business, shared with us his impressive collection of antique glass and allowed us to photograph some of the pieces while he patiently explained the finer points of their history and production.

The staff of Irreplaceable Artifacts assisted immensely. They offered helpful suggestions, did research, made contacts, took messages, and helped keep us sane.

And finally, we need to thank all of our friends and relatives who gave advice, lent props, and humored us through the entire process of preparing this book. A special hug for Ricardo and Gerhard, et pour Yves et Nicolas un gros bisous.

DESIGN CREDITS

Elaine Bedell at Studio E.B. (176); Barry Berg, Architect (153);

Walter E. Blum, Architect (36, 38, 54, 58, 82, 91, 103, 148, 171); Brendan Coburn, Architect (128);

Thérèse Coburn (77); Confluence (Art Consultant) (186, 189, 190); J. P. Friedman (44, 145);

Laura Gottwald & Associates, Inc. (40); Rob Greenberg (10, 79, 104, 114, 115, 118);

Nancy Karg, Architect (35); Mike Lebowitz (48); Lesser and Frisch, Inc. (61, 151); Tom Lowry (66);

Dana Nicholson Design (Cover, 68, 146, 147, 180); Pensis-Stolz, Inc. (184);

Yves P. Roger, Architect (71, 108); Rosenblum-Harb, Architects (80); SpecFin (48, 53);

Special Effects by Terri McRay (89, 110, 129); Arnold Syrop, Architect (116–17); Vi-Art (Art Consultant) (187, 188, 191UL); Larry Wentz, Architect (89, 142, 143); Zohreh Design, Inc. (112, 179)

PHOTOGRAPHY CREDITS

Principal photography by David Frazier. Additional photography provided as follows:

Photograph by Richard Nickel, courtsey of the Richard Nickel Committee, Chicago, Illinois (14).

Courtesy of The Library of Congress, Historic American Buildings Survey,
    photographer Cervin Robinson (16).

Photograph by Bill Rochert, courtesy of the Second City Comedy Club (17).

Courtesy of the the Historical Preservation Office, Department of Environmental Protection,
    State of New Jersey, with thanks to Vicky Goldberg (20).

Photograph by Salem Krieger (23).

The Brooklyn Museum (24).

New York City Landmarks Preservation Commission (32).

Courtesy of The Library of Congress, Historic American Buildings Survey,
    photographer Ned Goode (96).

Courtesy of The Library of Congress, Historic American Buildings Survey,
    photographer Jack Boucher (138).

Museum of the City of New York, The Bryon Collection (166).

INDEX

Page numbers in *italic* refer to captions.